Essential Knowledge for Teachers

Words of Wisdom

Barbara D. Culp

Glean knowledge and wisdom from the experiences of someone who has successfully traversed the roads of education. Written for educators and learners in all walks of the educational journey, *Words of Wisdom* provides a collection of guiding principles, practical advice, and encouraging words for both beginners and veterans in the world of education.

Other Titles in This Series

Vintage Knowledge for Principals: Keys to Enrich, Encourage, and Empower School Leaders and Empowering Today's Principals

Essential Knowledge for Teachers

Truths to Energize, Excite, and Engage Today's Teachers

Barbara D. Culp

ROWMAN & LITTLEFIELD
Lanham • Boulder • New York • London

Published by Rowman & Littlefield
A wholly owned subsidiary of The Rowman & Littlefield Publishing Group, Inc.
4501 Forbes Boulevard, Suite 200, Lanham, Maryland 20706
www.rowman.com

Unit A, Whitacre Mews, 26-34 Stannary Street, London SE11 4AB

British Library Cataloguing in Publication Information Available

Library of Congress Cataloguing-in-Publication Data

Name: Culp, Barbara D., 1947– author.
Title: Essential knowledge for teachers : truths to energize, excite, and engage today's teachers / Barbara D. Culp.
Description: Lanham : Rowman & Littlefield, a wholly owned subsidiary of The Rowman & Littlefield Publishing Group, Inc., [2017]
Identifiers: LCCN 2016032660 | ISBN 9781475831320 (pbk. : alk. paper)
Subjects: LCSH: Teaching. | Reflective teaching. | Teachers—Conduct of life.
Classification: LCC LB1025.3 .C855 2017 | DDC 371.102—dc23
LC record available at https://lccn.loc.gov/2016032660

♾™ The paper used in this publication meets the minimum requirements of American National Standard for Information Sciences—Permanence of Paper for Printed Library Materials, ANSI/NISO Z39.48-1992.

Printed in the United States of America

This book is dedicated to my uniquely talented and super smart youngest sister, Dr. B. Annette Daughtry, also known as Ain Modeira Baberinwa, who has devoted her life to bringing out the best in the thousands of students whose lives she touched as a mathematics teacher. Annette gives freely and students receive gladly the knowledge and wisdom she has to offer.
I'm glad God chose Annette to be one of my sisters!

"Teachers who inspire realize there will always be rocks in the road ahead of us.

There will be stumbling blocks or stepping stones; it all depends on how we use them."

~Anonymous

Contents

Foreword

Besides being very flattered that the author would ask me to write this foreword, I can't think of a better title for this book, *Essential Knowledge for Teachers: Truths to Energize, Excite, and Engage Today's Teachers*. As the Dean of the College of Education, I have never seen a more compact and beautifully written book of wisdom to guide veteran teachers and inspire novice teachers. Dr. Culp shares genuine pearls from her long and successful career as an educator.

The book is arranged in four sections: community, parents, teachers, and ends with a section on always a teacher. It can be read in a single` sitting or picked up and put down when time allows. The feeling of genuine appreciation of the role of teachers and their awesome responsibility toward students is the overwhelming takeaway. Dr. Culp has a unique way of offering advice and motivating principles which tug at the heartstring of the reader and move them to excellence.

Dr. Culp no doubt shares the wisdom of William Butler Yeats who said, "Education is not the filling of a pail, but the lighting of a fire." Curl up and enjoy!

Dr. Sandra L. Leslie
Dean, College of Education
Brenau University

Preface

Teachers show students how to unlock information in a way that maximizes learning. In today's educational landscape, that means constantly learning how to use new tools, locating new resources, and always looking forward to the brightest future!

To succeed, you need to identify each student's strengths and weaknesses, build study skills, encourage engagement, unlock learning blocks, and prepare students for college and careers. The training and development you've already undergone have made you an instructional specialist. You know how to engage students, maintain their focus, and develop the kinds of activities that maximize academic performance.

Your dedication, demonstrated by your total focus and unwavering attention, proves that the welfare of your students is your top priority. That includes acting as a guide. You set high expectations and know that every student, no matter where they are when they first arrive in your classroom, can succeed! Along the way you'll hold many hands, wipe a few tears, and offer comfort and praise.

Some of your students will break your heart; others will burnish your teaching star until it shines like a supernova! No matter what you encounter, you are not alone. A host of teachers have come before you, and an army of recruits is learning how to step in after you leave. You are part of an unbroken chain of academic excellence our country values enough to make mandatory for all children. The work is hard, the hours are long. A lot is asked of you … and a lot is returned.

The easy smiles of a class comfortable with your leadership return to you. The pride in a parent's eyes feeds you. The trust of administrators who allow you to take the lead empowers you. The camaraderie of your peers and the moments they reach out for help or to offer assistance support you. All these moments swirl together in the kaleidoscope of your days. Every shining bit is your medal and your maker. They are your nourishment and your reward. Hold that knowledge close. Keep it in your heart. Make others say, "Wow!"

Acknowledgments

From the beginning of time, man has taught man. The process was passed down for generations and evolved into one of the most necessary professions in the world. Society's advancements can be attributed to the teaching and training of its citizenry. From among those gifted with the most knowledge arose teachers as we know them today. They nurture as they pass on knowledge and instill wisdom in the children they touch.

This book celebrates the teacher. *Essential Knowledge for Teachers: Truths to Energize, Excite, and Engage Today's Teachers* is dedicated to the individuals worldwide who give their all without a thought for themselves. They dedicate their lives to a form of service that has no expiration date. Many knew early on that their path would lead to the classroom. Because they treat every person with love and compassion, they inspire others to follow in their footsteps.

These courageous and necessary champions of knowledge impel a lifelong thirst for learning. With guidance, students become who their maker designed them to be. The more they learn, the more our society advances. Bravo to teachers everywhere for the awesome job they do grooming our children to uphold important norms and mores!

Teaching is an awesome responsibility. Continue to do it so well that no one living, dead, or yet to be born can do it better. Your patience, caring, and strong desire to see all children achieve their full potential is your constant gift to mankind. WOW, to be called a teacher!

Introduction

Teachers are the historians, interpreters, and transmitters of knowledge. They are agents of change who nurture the minds of our newest generations. Every day, they serve as role models, leaders, and the caretakers of our future. Their primary job is to pass down knowledge so that our youth become strong intellectual citizens. Along the way, they provide socioemotional lessons that help young adults integrate into our society.

For 15 years, I worked hard every day to make a difference in the classroom. The students I taught went on to college and took up professional jobs. The ones who decided not to pursue college or high-paying careers are making their marks as parents, craftsmen, and artists. Each child who passed over the threshold of my classroom was preordained to connect with me. My job was to give them everything they needed for that year.

If you're a teacher, you likely feel much the same way. Your training and development has made you an instructional specialist. You locate the resources your students need to engage fully with their lessons, and you plan each day's activities to maximize academic success. You tailor your instructional methods to the needs of every student according to their background, their current abilities, and their potential.

Equally important is your role as guide. You help young people navigate the turbulent waters of their lives. You set high expectations, assume that everyone can advance in their education, and don't allow underachievers to fall through the cracks. Through context and questions, you allow students to develop new perspectives and creative ideas. And because teamwork is a must, you encourage parents, peers, and the larger community to become involved.

Finally, you are a student's surrogate parent and adult friend. You form strong relationships to show them how much you care. For some children, you are the most (perhaps the only) stable adult in their lives. For others, you are yet another example of the kind of adult they can become. You might never be a rock star but you are always a guiding light!

In this book, we'll look at your role as a teacher and the wisdom you can provide to students, parents, peers, and administrators. Tips for staying relevant, effective, and on top of your game will be provided. Initiatives that have proven successful will be offered. Best of all, we'll celebrate the special place you claim in the lives of the thousands of children you'll touch during your career.

Essential Knowledge: Keys to Energize, Excite, and Engage Today's Teachers is divided into three categories: Essential Knowledge for Your Community, Essential Knowledge for Your Classroom, and Essential Knowledge for Yourself. Within each section, individual entries define a specific type of wisdom, delineate its benefits, and provide at least one example. Specific tips that are easy to implement show you how to make the wisdom work in your classroom. This book can be read straight through or in sections. At any time, you can read a random entry to discover what waits!

My experience in the academic realm spans 43 years. For 15 of those years, I taught preschool, elementary and middle grades before being promoted to principal. Even after I retired, I missed my chosen profession so much I couldn't stay away. So I founded Amyra Tutorial, a program that helps students in the nation's schools, and began writing a series about educational wisdom. The wisdom you hold in your hands distills all that experience into a compact format that runs as deep as a river.

What will you discover today? Turn the page and say, "WOW!"

Part I

Essential Knowledge for the Community

GENUINE LOVE

Genuine love is the nucleus around which a teacher's day revolves.

Genuine love generates powerful benefits. When students feel nurtured in the classroom, they respond in kind. Behavior improves, attendance grows more stable, and incidents of tardiness decrease. And since you care about everything a student is and everything they can become, they naturally strive to fulfill all their potential!

The vehicle through which you can convey *genuine love* is already a part of your classroom. The rules that govern how students behave and the expectations you've laid out communicate how deeply you care. When you expect a student to arrive on time, you communicate that the depth of learning they experience matters. You also prove to the rest of the students that their time is as valuable as yours … and that their education is also important.

Convey *genuine love* by treating students of every age with fairness and respect. When every student is given the same opportunity to succeed … as well as the same guidance when they fall short … they recognize that your love doesn't play favorites. They are all equal in your eyes. Their confidence and self-worth rise! Bolstered by that support, they strive to reach the bars you set.

BE A CHEERLEADER

Be a cheerleader means you praise publically and discipline privately … and not only with your students!

Being a cheerleader is never more important than at school. Calling out a student's accomplishments enhances their confidence and inspires other students to achieve. Peers and even administrators discover that you pay attention to their actions and feel supported. Parents realize that your involvement extends beyond the classroom. And by ensuring that any discussion of negative activities happens in private, you show everyone that you respect them.

Being a cheerleader creates a feedback loop that supports you! Teachers at one school created a Sunshine Fund to purchase little gifts that say, "We care." A Sunshine Fund can also be used to recognize individuals who go above and beyond. No matter how your school uses this type of fund, it builds cohesion in the school community … and contributors feel great!

Being a cheerleader isn't always simple, especially when a student acts inappropriately in the classroom. The behavior has to be addressed right away but you also want to shield them from taunts by their fellow students. During class, firmly stop the misbehavior and remind the student of the rules. If necessary, follow up later when the class is working on individual assignments or in groups. Step into the doorway to share a few quiet words to make your point. And if you ever have issues during a meeting with adults, the same process applies!

POSITIVE PROFESSIONALISM

Positive professionalism blends excellent skills with the polite demeanor that will serve your career.

Positive professionalism is one of a teacher's greatest assets. It blends training and abilities with the polished behavior of a career professional. When you display positive professionalism, you inspire trust in the entire school community. People recognize that you are capable and confident in your service. Others become more willing to help, your ideas are heard more easily … and in difficult times, you'll be given the benefit of the doubt.

Positive professionalism has never been more important than it is today. Social issues like drugs and teen pregnancy, tragic school shootings, and concerns about predators have placed teachers under a magnifying glass. A research paper for Elsevier Science Ltd. found that over the last several decades, teachers in every country are operating under an increasing number of external demands. How they are viewed is increasingly dependent on how others perceive them. Positive professionalism eliminates any concerns over your ability to create a safe and inspiring educational environment.

Positive professionalism isn't a set of activities; instead, it's about inner strength. When you recognize the extent of your training and wisdom, you project a confident, capable demeanor that inspires trust. By treating others with courtesy—even when they don't offer you the same—you broadcast sterling professionalism. And when you enhance your demeanor by staying focused on potentials and opportunities, you become a truly positive professional.

PARENT POWER!

Parent power recognizes that parents can—and should—be a teacher's best ally.

Parent power helps you build powerful educational alliances. Parents are the ultimate authority figures in a student's life, and so can enforce positive behaviors and habits. Their deeply emotional connection to their children can be an avenue for breakthroughs that are difficult to achieve in school. And since they have lives off campus, each parent can become a champion for you and your school in the community.

Parent power has a profound effect when a student is troubled. The National Alliance on Mental Illness (NAMI) reports that suicide is the second leading cause of death among teens. Although 20 percent of children experience mental health issues, only 20 percent of them actually receive help. When parents and teachers watch for signs and symptoms, they can get the child (and the family) help more quickly. And when students are supported this way, the learning environment becomes more stable.

Enhance *parent power* by allowing parents to ask as many questions as they like whenever you connect with them. Encouraging communication builds trust that you'll respond to new ideas or issues. Reach out to parents individually with a quick e-mail, text, or call. By connecting with one parent every day, you'll provide individual attention to every parent. When combined with your usual newsletters, social media updates and school meetings, that one extra step will create real allies you can call on.

COLLABORATE

Collaborate with other teachers to supercharge academic achievement!

In a study of more than a thousand fourth- and fifth-grade teachers in New York City, researcher Carrie Leana found that *collaboration* created higher gains in student achievement. Collaboration also enhances trust among teachers, ensuring that your network of peers provides a safe, secure place where you can excel.

Collaborating is the foundation of a strong relationship with colleagues. When you are connected to your peers, you feel supported. When you share planning time with other teachers, you'll share tips and techniques while learning new tricks to make your job easier. And by sharing triumphs and trials, you'll relieve stress and revel in the milestones that make your efforts so very worthwhile.

Collaborate in ways large and small. If your school system doesn't have a set time when you can gather with other teachers, ask for some of the professional development time to be set aside for this activity. Use social media, text messaging and e-mail to send quick notes to others in your network. Pop into other classrooms between periods or before and after school. If you spend a minute or two with a different teacher every day of the week, you'll make them feel supported and gather a strong group around you!

TEACH THE PARENTS

Teach the parents how they can support your classroom objectives.

Teaching parents creates a strong parent-teacher dynamic. It ensures that the adults are aware of classroom activities and school goals as well as how their own efforts impact education. Finally, teaching parents benefits the school community by encouraging active involvement.

One excellent outcome from *teaching parents* is found with social skills. Today's educational environment respects the culturally and linguistically diverse backgrounds that make up our society. Many students at risk of academic failure have poor social skills, so it's especially important to have an impact in the home. Learning Disabilities, an online resource for educators, believes that collaboration between educators and sparents creates a much better outcome for prosocial skills.

Teach parents which skills to promote by sharing information in newsletters or on social media. Provide fact-based information about the benefits of engaging in educational games. Reinforce these prompts by following up with links to free educational games or family-friendly TV shows. Follow up again with quotes from the show or share your own scores on an educational game. Every update generates new attention to the same area and improves the chances that parents will take these lessons to heart!

MANNERS MATTER

Manners matter because they stabilize the classroom environment and enhance socioemotional development.

Manners matter anytime a group of people come together for a common purpose … especially when those individuals are young! Good manners ensure that everyone treats their peers and you with respect. It allows the lesson plan to flow smoothly and keeps attention focused on education.

Manners matter to kids as much as adults. Savannah Shaw, an etiquette coach and international business consultant, notes that well-mannered kids are more liked by their peers and grow up to become better leaders. Cindy Post Senning, Ed. D. and director of the Emily Post Institute, notes, "Manners are just social behaviors that help us build and strengthen relationships." The social-emotional development that good manners promote will have an impact long after students leave your classroom.

Teach that *manners matter* by encouraging the use of "please" and "thank you" with other students as well as adults. No one is allowed to rummage through someone else's backpacks or desks, and the communal space should be honored by assigning cleaning and straightening tasks on a rotating basis. Eye rolling, scoffing and sighing are off limits when someone else is speaking! Respect for others develops respect for themselves … and that creates a nurturing, supportive environment.

THE DIFFERENCE IS YOU

The difference is you is the founding truth of every teacher's job.

The difference is you highlights the impact you have in every student's life. It reminds you that your presence in the classroom, the care you take treating every child as an individual, and the vision you hold for their future makes a difference. Every time you step into the classroom, the difference in your students' lives is you.

The difference is you has a lifelong impact. Michele Dunaway, an English teacher in St. Charles, Missouri, told Teachers at Work that she keeps in contact with many of her former students through social media. She taught some of those students as long ago as 1993, and every update reminds her why she chose to teach. Even when times get tough, those connections prove that she makes a difference!

Signs that *the difference is you* are all around. When students ask questions, you've opened up their curiosity and engaged their intellect. Your students utilize the skills and abilities they already have to create something new because you encouraged their confidence. When young minds engage with the curriculum, you've made the lessons exciting and relevant to their worlds. And every time you call on your strength, patience and endurance to manage a crisis, the difference is you!

LISTENING IS LEARNING

Listening is learning when you allow students, teachers, and peers to make you more effective and efficient.

Listening is learning in any human relationship. Listening makes people feel heard and shores up their self-worth. Listening allows you to assess what an individual needs as well as where they're coming from. Listening conveys respect and builds trust. Listening deeply improves your recall of what you've heard, which makes your job easier!

Listening is learning is more than passively accepting someone's words. Eric Glover, associate professor of educational leadership and policy analysis at East Tennessee State University, notes that debate and dialogue are an important part of listening. When individuals engage with each other, they bring wisdom and creative solutions to the table. A simple thought can become a powerful new pathway for the school. An everyday habit can become a standard procedure that lightens a coworker's load. And, of course, students recognize that their thoughts and ideas count!

Listen to learn by opening yourself up to new thoughts and ideas. Withhold judgment while listening, and allow the speaker to finish before responding. Then interpret what has been said while remembering that words and phrases can mean different things to different people. Empower students to take charge of their education by allowing them to find answers to everyday problems!

BE A ROLE MODEL

Be a role model for students and peers to lift your school and your community!

Being a role model makes a gift of your best self to the children, parents, teachers and administrators with whom you work. You provide young people with a picture of the kind of person they could become. You display the wisdom that encourages parents to follow your lead. And you encourage your coworkers to put in their own best effort.

Being a role model has a huge impact in the classroom, and in more ways than you might think. Take, for instance, the difficulty in encouraging girls to believe in their abilities in science, technology, engineering and mathematics (STEM). In a paper for the University of Washington, Sapna Cheryan found that a role model's gender did not influence how girls judged their ability to succeed in STEM. Both male and female teachers can encourage them to explore these career fields.

You don't have to preach morals or values to *be a role model.* Instead, self-discipline and self-control have a much greater impact. When you combine these qualities with your passion and excitement for teaching and learning, you become a role model everyone can turn to.

INTEGRATE INTEGRITY

Integrating integrity weaves your moral principles into a unified attitude.

Integrating integrity allows your personal values to become the framework for your days. When you integrate integrity, you act in a consistent manner that garners trust and goodwill. Your worldview clearly values honesty and authenticity, two of a teacher's most valuable assets.

When you *integrate integrity*, cheating, plagiarism, fabrication, and deception are banned in the classroom. Although students are usually the focus of this type of effort, the same goes for your peers and staff—cheating, fabrication, deception, and gossip aren't tolerated in the break room! When you stand by your moral principles and uphold what you know is right, others are much more likely to stand with you. It takes a village to raise a child but one voice speaking the truth can influence a community.

Integrate integrity with students by reviewing the school's honor code throughout the year. And don't just quote the rules; tell them how they will benefit from following those rules. When dealing with peers or coworkers who have lower standards, refuse to engage in gossip or scandal mongering. Recognize that there will be times when your framework doesn't match up to someone else's idea of integrity. So long as you are both working to advance the school and the students, differences are fine. You might even adjust your own values when you discover the value of someone else's framework!

RAPID RESPONSE

Rapid response means that you attend to all work-based communications in an appropriate timeframe.

Rapid response marks you as a true professional. It allows you to manage the many communications required by your position without overwhelming you or interfering with a productive work flow.

Rapid response pays off big in your relationships with parents. In this case, the first step is always to make a connection through calls or e-mails during the first week or two of school. This signals that the lines of communication are open, and allows you to introduce the social media pages parents can follow for regular updates … which itself eases your communications burden! Then, when individual parents initiate a call, e-mail or other contact, you're under much less pressure to respond immediately. They trust that you'll get back to them in a timely fashion because you've already made the first step.

Rapid response isn't about answering every call or e-mail within an hour. Instead, it's about managing the flow of communications. Items that require immediate action—disciplinary issues, falling grades and the like—should be given same-day turnarounds. Questions about upcoming events or activities can wait a few days, which allows you to blind copy everyone's questions with a single e-mail. When you want to share news about positive developments, host a casual get-together after school. Three get-togethers a year are enough to make parents feel supported and encourage the personal interactions that strengthen relationships.

BE REAL

Be real to connect with your students (as well as your peers) on a human level.

Being real makes your students more comfortable, which enhances academic performance, engagement, and behavior. Keeping yourself real connects you on a deeper level with your peers and even administrations. Parents want to know the people responsible for their children and trust individuals who present as stable, reliable individuals.

Being real is supported by Learning Forward. In a 2013 report, they noted that education has become burdened with data and statistics. The functional core, though, is found in the people who actually put in the work. They identified 14 parameters that implement deep and sustainable teaching methods, all of which relate to the human side of teaching!

Be real by engaging with your students on a human level. Know where they come from and what motivates them to learn. Give them the power to be responsible for themselves. Be as proud of your student's accomplishments as their parents! Recognize that even kids can have bad days. When you support them in good times and bad, you reach them on a real level.

CONSTANT CONTACT

Constant contact with parents ensures a cohesive front … and eliminates unpleasant surprises!

Constant contact allows parents to reinforce the skills and lessons their kids are learning. Your missives might alert them to strengths and weaknesses, likes and dislikes they had no idea existed! Students who know that their teachers communicate frequently with their parents act differently in school, so behaviors are better and their attention is more likely to be on you. Finally, constant contact constantly builds trust.

Steve Reifman, an elementary school teacher who is now an educational speaker, says *constant contact* connects teachers and parents in important ways. Parents can become a true ally in the educational process. Regular communication informs parents about the habits and expectations for class time, which can then be reinforced at home. Parents who are in touch become valuable resources by volunteering, donating materials, and providing other types of support.

Constant contact with parents takes a variety of forms. There are parent-teacher meetings, phone calls, and e-mails. You can also send home folders that showcase important lessons every week or once a month. When you ask parents to comment on the folders, you enhance the communication by making it a two-way street. Undertake a variety of methods to connect with every household!

DUTY TO WARN

Duty to warn reminds you to step up when you possess information that might be harmful to others if it's kept quiet.

Duty to warn is an unfortunate reality for teachers. Educators deal every day with children from a variety of backgrounds. Sometimes those kids are neglected, abused, or manipulated in ways that are harmful to their health and well-being. When you step forward and reveal this type of information, you help build a better life for the children involved.

Duty to warn is an integral part of the National Education Association's (NEA) code of ethics. While laws cover most of the situations related to abuse and neglect, the NEA's code includes areas that aren't as clear-cut. One of their principles prevents the suppression or distortion of subject matter children need to know. Another principle deals with the character of individuals entering the teaching profession; when people aren't suited for the job, they're hiding the fact that they won't make good teachers.

Duty to warn encompasses areas large and small. Don't withhold information from colleagues, administrators, parents, or students if the result will be in any detrimental way. Although this can be a very difficult and awkward choice, making it proves your unassailable character. Step up and speak out!

MENTOR OTHERS

Mentor others and give back by grooming preservice teachers.

Mentoring others recharges your enthusiasm with fresh faces eager to lead their own classes. It expands your network of peers and strengthens your support team. And when you mentor a preservice teacher, you help them avoid pitfalls by sharing the wisdom you've gained over the years … which in turn helps their students!

The University of Texas found that *mentoring others* boosts the confidence of preservice and novice teachers. Individuals who acted as mentors found the activity and the new relationships fulfilling. The impact was so profound that the study proposed that teacher and administrator preparation programs nationwide should place a much greater emphasis on mentoring!

Mentor others by listening to their concerns and sharing the wisdom you've gained. Observe classroom performance if possible and pay particular attention to body language. Whenever you provide feedback, be sure to comment on your mentee's strengths. Bolster their confidence so they can improve their weaknesses in ways you develop together. And remember that your goal is to create a self-sufficient teacher. Over time, your mentoring relationship will gradually become one shared by equals.

COCURRICULAR ACTIVITIES

Cocurricular activities enhance academic results.

Cocurricular activities ensure that every student and teacher brings a broad base of understanding to school. When you champion these activities, you'll enhance the cultural, social, and intellectual development of every student. When you pursue them yourself and encourage your peers to join you, the school bursts with savvy, smart teachers who can give the kids their best!

Cocurricular activities benefit everyone. Students support their learning when they develop emotionally, physically, and morally. Positive perspectives are developed hand in hand with budding personalities, so the experiences enhance behavior. For the adults in charge, cocurricular activities provide spiritual growth, solidify positive character traits, and help them become more fluent educators.

Support *cocurricular activities* by supporting arts and sports. Whenever possible, integrate hands-on creative elements into your lessons. Consider book binding as a part of writing or reading units, clay modeling for sciences, or first-aid techniques in biology. Lead optional field trips on days when families can join you at a local karate or swim center for a free session. Build an events calendar where everyone at the school can post cocurricular activities they discover to really spread the wealth!

ENCOURAGE COLLEGE

Encourage college no matter how old your students might be ... it's never too early or too late!

Encourage college at every age and in every classroom. You might be the first adult in a student's life to suggest that he or she can succeed on that path. Always extend the conversation to the parents. Those in lower economic brackets might give up on sending their kids before they explore all the options, so you could make a big impact in a family's life!

Encouraging college in middle-grade students has received a lot more attention from governmental, educational, and social organizations lately. There is a much greater recognition nowadays that high school and college readiness needs to be encouraged early. A United Way program conducted in 2014 encouraged college early. It cut the number of school dropouts in half and improved college-readiness rates in all nine communities where it was tested!

Encourage college in your students by calling on volunteers to provide empowerment workshops and career planning. Invite parents to help set up the programs or even attend! Get students to present workshops they've created as part of an assignment. A peer culture that supports college aspirations fuels dreams for the future.

REFLECTIVE INTERACTION

Reflective interaction enhances your relationships with students, peers, parents, and administrators.

Reflective interaction builds the deep and meaningful connections that create strong, long-lasting relationships. No matter how busy you are, reflective interaction generates positive results by enhancing even brief interactions!

Reflective interaction works! Study after study has found that educational outcomes are higher when administrative staff are tied into their teachers, when teachers interact as peers, and when students and parents have a rapport with teachers. Socioemotional learning soars, the academic environment becomes more peaceful, and the larger community engages more. With all these benefits, why wouldn't you interact reflectively?

Practice *reflective interaction* by observing a classroom lead by a teacher one or more grades above or below your own level. Keep notes on parents: where they work, the obstacles they face, and how their situations change over time. Be aware that administrators are human beings with lives outside of school. And recognize that your students have goals, aspirations, and desires as unique as their young minds. Honor the fullness of each person and you'll automatically interact in a thoughtful, reflective manner!

MAP THE BOUNDARIES

Mapping the boundaries allows you to reach for more because you know exactly where the limits lie.

Mapping the boundaries is all about pushing limits ... your own, those of your students, and even the limits of parents and administrators. When you know where different people begin to falter, you're better able to help them achieve. By knowing your own boundaries, you'll move past them in a series of small steps or in a single giant leap.

Mapping the boundaries is an activity you already perform for your students. Your constant assessment of their ability levels, their preferred learning modes, and their academic weaknesses guide your daily efforts. When you apply the same assessments to your peers and yourself, a world of opportunities opens up. Guide yourself to new heights, and you'll inspire your peers to do the same!

Map the boundaries of your peers by observing how they handle everyday stress. If they constantly seem unsettled when interacting with parents, are they dealing with difficult individuals, or do they need better communication skills? If some teachers seem constantly exhausted, are they overwhelmed by their workload or could they become more efficient planners? When you map their boundaries, you're in a better position to offer a helping hand.

EXPLORE THE ICEBERG

Explore the iceberg because what's on the surface is only a small percentage of the whole.

Exploring the iceberg takes you deep into the curriculum, the students, and your school. Educational mandates are simply the nuclei around which a universe of possible lessons rotates. Students, although young, are human beings driven by individual passions and motivations. The school is a single point in the broader community as well as the nation. Exploring all that potential brings the world into your classroom!

When students *explore the iceberg* by socializing and cooperating with many other students, they recognize that all their peers are pursuing a common goal. Teachers who reach across subjects to integrate other ideas and concepts into their lessons provide students with a systemic academic view. And when you reach out to educators who teach other grades or subjects, you build a web of relationships that run as deep as a well!

Explore the iceberg by getting to know people in ways that expand beyond academic concerns. Discover what special skills parents might offer the school, students who are not their children, and each other. Recognize that your peers go deeper than the faces they present at work, and share your own depths while building relationships. Exploring the iceberg can—and should—be a consistent part of your career!

INTUIT

Intuit how others think and feel to stay ahead of the game.

Every classroom is filled with young people who *intuit* more often than they apply critical thinking. Children are guided by their emotions … which can make things difficult. When adults judiciously apply their intuition, they respond more quickly, develop deeper relationships, and stay ahead of events!

Faculty Focus, a collection of teaching strategies from Magna Publications, reports that teachers rely on their *intuition* every day. Whenever you adjust a lesson plan on the fly, you're calling on your intuition. You recognize in the present moment that something isn't working. Perhaps the students don't grasp the lesson or they simply aren't engaged. You pick up the signals and, using an inner guide based on experiences and wisdom, you change your procedures to help them understand and reengage.

Know that *intuition* isn't a fuzzy approach based only on emotions. Instead, it's a message that arises from your subconscious, the place where all your experiences as an educator and leader are stored. After years of work and development, you are able to intuit what the class needs, what each student needs, and what your school needs. Whenever you "have a feeling" that something isn't working, trust your intuition! It's based on wisdom so ingrained that it can't be explained or quantified.

CHOOSE CIVILITY

Choose civility to manage any situation from overwrought students to overjoyed parents.

Choosing civility marks you as the consummate professional. When you interact with individuals in a way that is honest, thoughtful, and balanced, you'll tamp down hot tempers and stabilize youthful impulsiveness. You'll keep the lines of communication open no matter what! People will trust you not only for your skills as an educator but also for your skills in managing relationships.

Schools have long *chosen civility* as a core component of their makeup. Civility is based on membership in a community, working together, and consideration for everyone involved. In return, individuals who choose civility gain a set of rights (and responsibilities). More than mere politeness, civility in schools respects the people, the facility, and the goals of education.

Choose civility by maintaining a calm demeanor in every situation. The beginning of the year starts with politeness between strangers; as the year progresses, that same politeness strengthens relationships within the school community. Be aware of the goals of others, maintain control of your own words and emotions, offer empathy to those in need, and respect the goals of the school. When you model these four behaviors, you inspire everyone around you to choose civility. And that works for the entire academic community!

CALL ON CHARISMA

Call on charisma to develop the qualities of a born leader.

Calling on charisma is a classroom requirement. Students shouldn't just listen to you ... they should want to listen! Once this dynamic appears, students feel important in your presence. They are motivated to follow your directions, engage with the lessons, and achieve more. By expanding that charisma beyond the classroom, you'll build better relationships with peers, administrators, and parents.

Julia G. Thompson, a best-selling author and educator, says that *calling on charisma* is a skill that can be learned. Too often charisma is discussed as something people are born with or as a personality trait. Really, though, it's quite simple. Thompson does note that efforts to become charismatic have to be applied every day. Since it's actually a simple process, your charisma can grow all year long!

Call on charisma by mimicking a teacher who exemplifies charisma. This gives you an internal model to build on as you develop your own charisma. Thompson notes that demeanor is half the battle, so smile often! Overlook whatever small flaws you can in your students. They'll learn over time to read your body language and, as they become drawn to you, they will modify their own behaviors to eliminate those small annoyances. Ask questions so that students have the opportunity to share something about themselves. They'll feel more connected and important in your eyes!

RADIATE LOVE

Radiating love transforms the classroom with the true resonance of joy.

Radiating love enhances your relationships with the people around you and the place where you are. When you radiate love to your school community, you allow them to feel the depth of joy your profession provides. When you apply that same action to the school's facilities, special events and ongoing programs, you create a feedback loop that fuels an ever-growing well of joy in yourself!

Radiating love brings joy into the academic environment. Steven Wolk, an assistant professor of teacher education at Northeastern Illinois University, points out that joy isn't the same thing as fun. With joy, educators can capture students' minds, hearts, and souls. Pleasure in learning, creative outlets, inviting schools, and yes, even having fun, all create joy.

Radiate love for everything you do. No matter how severe the budget cuts, love the space you're in because it is truly the best your district can offer. Love your peers because even when they're struggling, they are putting in their best effort. Love the parents because even in the midst of their busy lives, they pay attention to their children's academic achievement. Always, always radiate love for yourself! You're a very special person who has answered a very special calling. That joy is boundless!

STUDENTS LEAD THE WAY

Students lead the way to the best teaching methods!

By allowing *students to lead the way*, you locate the most effective teaching methods. The variety of ability levels will all be served equally when you follow this lead. Students who struggle in other classrooms will be less likely to fall behind. Kids who display advanced abilities won't be so bored they zone out or misbehave. Your classroom will become a hive of academic activity that inspires and encourages success for all!

Students lead the way by demonstrating learning styles and aptitudes. The ones who listen intently often prefer to learn through auditory input. Those who tend to read quietly in the corner are often visual learners. The chatty ones frequently work out new challenges by organizing their thoughts verbally, while the kids who can't sit still probably prefer kinesthetic (hands-on) lessons.

Allow *students to lead the way* by observing their response to lessons, activities, and assignments. You'll quickly figure out their preferred learning modes and can set up group activities accordingly. When all your lessons incorporate a little from each learning method, you'll enhance the retention rates for your entire classroom.

Part II

Essential Knowledge for Your Classroom

PARENT EVERY CHILD

Parenting every child treats every student as if they were your son or daughter.

Parenting every child generates a stable rapport between you and your students. This wisdom generates a strong positive influence on academic and socioemotional development. Every advance made by the student becomes a triumph validated by someone who is important to them … their teacher!

Parenting every child is a natural extension of what teachers do in the classroom. By shepherding youth through whatever turmoil their age entails, you provide them with a valuable measuring stick against which they can judge their progress. You become an anchor in their lives, a person they trust. You're someone who listens and who steps in whenever that becomes necessary. You expand in their eyes … and in their hearts.

Parent every child by discussing inappropriate behavior in a firm yet caring manner. Validate good behavior when it is displayed regularly. Recognize outstanding efforts as well as the steady steps toward different milestones. Get to know their likes and dislikes, laugh at their jokes between classes, and encourage them to reach higher. When you parent every child, you become something more than their parent … you become their role model!

PROBLEM-SOLVING STUDENTS

Problem-solving students are ones who have learned how to create their own solutions.

Problem-solving students are a boon to your classroom and your school. When you teach this essential skill, students become more independent. They are able to work longer and perform more tasks without asking for input or assistance. They become more sensitive to the challenges others face and are more eager to help their peers. The patience they learn as they work through their own issues helps them become more patient and kind outside your classroom, which expands the benefits to the entire community.

Ken Watanabe, a global management consultant, thinks that *problem-solving students* are so critical he now teaches children these skills. Students who know how to solve their own issues display enhanced learning skills. They also demonstrate ownership of issues that otherwise might make them retreat into passivity. This engagement deepens understanding, which enhances their ability to tackle challenges of all types.

Create a classroom filled with *problem-solving students* by selecting a common challenge. Divide the class into small groups, so every student can engage with the problem directly. Ask each group to discuss one aspect of the challenge … when they notice it, for example, or what seems to be the cause. When each student presents one way to handle the issue, the entire class benefits!

BOOK 'EM!

Book 'em records details, so you can interpret student achievements, help parents help their children, and deliver the results administrators need.

Book 'em allows you to recognize each student's strengths and weaknesses. Once you're aware of those areas, you can track how individuals respond to different assignments and improve their academic performance. Sharing these notes with parents provides concrete ideas about what they can do at home. All this data becomes valuable to administrators who report on the school's initiatives and progress.

Book 'em is all about record keeping. Most schools require that you keep records on tardies and absences, homework, and class work. *School Talk* magazine reported that some teachers require students to record their assignments. One group recorded the titles and authors of the books they'd read, rated the difficulty of the text, noted the genre, and listed the reading strategies they used. When those journals were applied across the curriculum, students discovered new things about themselves!

Book 'em becomes much easier when you integrate digital programs. Use Google's calendar or a different app to set up a master schedule for your lesson plan. Block out specific times for each unit then break those down according to different aspects of the curriculum. You can easily make notes every day. As a bonus, you can reuse or adapt the same calendar for the following academic year!

SUPPORT SPECIALNESS

Support specialness in every child … even when their unique ability or trait isn't directly related to academic achievement.

When you *support specialness,* you single out a student's strength. In an environment where children might feel like they're constantly failing, discovering that they have a valuable skill improves their confidence. Your relationship with each student grows stronger because you see them as individuals.

Supporting specialness goes hand in hand with differentiated instruction. DI methodologies expose students to new techniques, encourage peer assistance, and allow each child to learn at their own pace. The approach also harnesses preferred learning modes, utilizes creative talents, and inspires engagement to create an upward spiral of success. Almost any DI method you try will help you promote the specialness in each child.

Support specialness by turning "flaws" into skills. A child who is easily distracted is probably very inquisitive and can lead the class into new activities. Ones who tend to be flustered by new activities are likely very sensitive and can be emotionally supportive of their peers. The shy child who reads a lot might share a treasure trove of stories they've dreamed up on their own. When you call out these special traits and integrate them into the lesson, every child recognizes their own specialness!

TEACH GENTLY

Teaching gently recognizes that poor behavior is a symptom rather than a problem.

When you *teach gently,* you allow students who might have no other adult role models to feel safe with you. A teacher who is gentle even with discipline provides a connection that is loving and nurturing. You prove that, no matter what, your respect and care for that child is unconditional.

Teaching gently began in the 1980s when John McGee developed a method for those with intellectual challenges and behavioral issues. This method was founded in the idea that every person needs to be connected to another person, that gentle teaching benefits students, their classrooms, and the larger community. When you expand these principles to every student, you're able to handle fragile, developing psyches with compassion.

Teach gently by remembering, first and foremost, that unwanted behaviors are symptoms of a deeper problem. Students might be frustrated by their inability to complete a task or by what they perceive as their continuous failures. Students might sabotage group activities by not participating or by interfering with others. Show such students that the grades others receive aren't important. … It's only important that they make progress in their own abilities. When you teach gently, you reach children on a deep level that carries far beyond the classroom.

ARRIVE EARLY

Arrive early to the plans you've developed to ensure that your efforts progress smoothly.

Arriving early allows you to head off issues before they materialize. As you prepare for each new week, month, or quarter, a quick review allows you to assess the status of your plans. Things change. By reviewing your plans early, you can make small adjustments that will reap big rewards.

Arriving early helps you in a practical and a psychological way. The American Library Association breaks teacher planning down into: visualizing the future, inventorying the necessary steps, and then constructing a framework in which those actions can succeed. Interestingly, goals play only a minor role. Instead, the environment, the social atmosphere of the classroom, and the context are much more important. Arriving early generates a feeling of control that serves teachers at every level!

Arrive early by setting up your calendar before the academic year begins. Consider the curriculum, the usual mix of student abilities, and the backgrounds from which the children come. After you've met your new students, you can adjust the curriculum to better serve their needs. Each Friday, review the upcoming week's activities and modify the plan on the basis of here and now. When you arrive early, your workload becomes easier to handle and the results become more powerful.

CHALLENGE CHAMPIONS

Challenge champions launches every student down a path paved with their own best effort.

Challenge champions makes every student in your classroom a champion. From low performers to those who make top grades seem easy, every child can achieve new heights with positive, proactive guidance. They gain confidence, test scores rise, and you'll be an integral part of your school's national ranking!

Challenge champions utilizes the passions every individual has to achieve … even in areas that don't hold much appeal for them. A high-school teacher in Sacramento, California, who coauthored *The ESL/ELL Teacher's Survival Guide*, overcame a student's refusal to write an essay by tapping into his love of football and video games. When the student was told he could write about either topic, he ended up writing essays about both!

Challenge champions in your classroom. Always convey positive support for students' efforts, especially when they're working on something they don't like. Your support might help them stay engaged long enough to discover an aspect they hadn't considered before. Be flexible with assignments so you can tap into individual passions. And make your efforts consistent. Try every day to integrate challenges, and soon your classroom will overflow with champions!

HIGH RISK EQUALS HIGH REWARD

High risk equals high reward allows you to manage students who are in bad circumstances for their own best results.

The attitude that *high risk equals high reward* has a huge impact on the lives of the children who are the most in need. By providing a safe, stable environment, you make your classroom a place where kids can escape their home environments. When you demonstrate that you are balanced and in control of your emotions, you prove that there are people in authority who can be trusted.

High risk equals high reward isn't about solving the child's problems. It is about ameliorating the symptoms while they're with you. Too often, kids who deal with alcohol or drug abuse in the home, AWOL parents, and other types of neglect end up with a reputation as "bad students." When you recognize that acting out, a sullen affect, or a refusal to complete assignments are all cries for help, you can prove that the classroom is a nurturing environment where they can thrive.

High risk equals high reward is a slow, consistent process. Treat every child as equals among their peers. Grant them the respect you give adults. Communicate that your expectations aren't lower just because their parents aren't supportive. ... You know they're capable of more, and your confidence in their abilities builds their confidence! Meet them where they stand and then lead them to the fullness of who they can be.

PATIENCE EQUALS PERSISTENCE

Patience equals persistence is the formula that unlocks consistent, long-term success.

Patience equals persistence gives you a one-step process that propels you to teaching success. When you employ patience in your classroom, you have the ability to endure—and even thrive—during the most challenging situations. Every time your patience takes you through a difficult event, you emerge with your ability to move forward intact. You will head forever into the future!

Patience equals persistence is a heroic activity. Julius Caesar said, "It is easier to find men who will volunteer to die, than to find those who are willing to endure pain with patience." And as any teacher can tell you, the educational realm is fraught with potentially painful moments! Inflexible mandates, scurrilous students, and unreasonable parents can test the best of us. In every case, call on the wisdom that this too shall pass. You'll continue to serve in a spotlessly professional way.

Patience equals persistence, and it shifts your perspective. When a potentially frustrating situation occurs, patience helps you remember the bigger picture. A wise teacher knows that behavioral issues, unwieldy demands, and inflexible rules are part of the typical school environment.

By staying focused on academic success, you automatically find the best path forward … even when the way seems snarled with brambles!

SMARTPHONES ON

Smartphones on utilizes technology in the classroom.

Smartphones on enhances productivity and efficiency. Importantly, smartphones can also be used to organize lessons and assess learning. Apps and information available through the Internet can expand your curriculum without any impact on the school's budget. And because the youngest generations are raised with digital devices, students will automatically feel more confident with assignments because they're using a familiar device.

Smartphones on is supported by the National Education Association. Their advice and support column notes that one world history and AP government teacher quells nonacademic digital activities by roaming around the room. A reminder app pings students with upcoming due dates, and parents often sign up for the same notifications to help their children stay on track. The teacher has been "stunned" by how many students are now completing their homework!

Smartphones on can be implemented in nearly any classroom. Students who don't own a smartphone can be paired up with students who do. And because smartphones change the classroom dynamic from front-of-the-room lectures to a roaming, interactive model, teachers build better relationships with students and are able to respond immediately to difficulties. Smartphones can be a smart choice for your classroom!

GROUP FOR GREAT RESULTS

Group for great results uses various grouping patterns to optimize learning.

Group for great results considers the needs of individual students as well as the entire classroom. In addition to affecting how well children learn, the process builds relationships between students. Short-term groupings allow your class to reach specific goals in a faster, more effective manner!

Grouping for great results has been used for decades because it works. The Nebraska and Iowa Departments of Education note that grouping allows teachers and kids to target specific interests in a way that is tailored to student abilities. When you group kids who have the same needs together, you naturally reduce the effort needed to lift them out of their problem areas and set them on the path to success.

Group for great results is a flexible process. At times, you'll want the entire classroom to listen to the same information or participate in the same activity. At other times, you'll use large groups to tackle projects that have multiple components. Small groups are useful when you want to enhance the amount of support each child receives from peers. Groups benefit you by reducing your workload!

DIFFERENTIATE TO DELIVER

Differentiate to deliver pairs a variety of instructional strategies to students' abilities and interests.

Differentiate to deliver takes into account each student's learning style and level of readiness when preparing lesson plans. It helps students ranging from those with learning disabilities to ones who demonstrate high ability. Because the approach is flexible, it is perfectly suited to today's diverse classrooms and serves individuals from every sociocultural background.

Differentiate to deliver really started in the one-room schoolhouses that served our pioneers. When the Individuals with Disabilities Education Act (IDEA) was passed in 1975, the approach found supporters because it was quite effective with this particular group. In 2000, when No Child Left Behind became law, differentiated instruction came into the fullness of its current incarnation.

Differentiate to deliver bypasses the issues found with lecture-based instructional methods, the least effective of all choices. Content can be differentiated by referring to Bloom's Taxonomy, which categorizes different types of thinking skills. Then consider the learning style each child prefers and use that to determine who should write a report, create a graph, give an oral presentation, or build a model to demonstrate lesson mastery. When you differentiate, you deliver on state and federal mandates!

KNOW EACH STUDENT

Knowing each student provides you with the information you need to connect with each child.

Knowing each student allows you to understand the behaviors and personality traits that impact the classroom environment. Today's schools are melting pots of individuals from every conceivable social, economic, and cultural background. When you know the details about each of your children, you model tolerance and inclusion at your school.

Knowing each student has a profound impact on students with low self-esteem. In *Comprehensive Multicultural Education: Theory and Practice* (5th Edition), Christine Bennett, professor emerita at Indiana University, notes that a poor self-concept is one of the greatest obstacles to learning. A student's idea of how others perceive them is based on a lifetime of economic, cultural, educational, and social experiences. When you know what each student has faced yesterday, you help them grow today into the fullness of what they can become tomorrow!

Know each student by considering the twelve elements of culture set down by Cushner, McClelland, and Safford in *Human Diversity in Education:* ethnicity/nationality, social class, sex/gender, health, age, geographic region, sexuality, religion, social status, language, ability/disability, and race. Have students write about their cultural identities for an assignment early in the year. The information they'll reveal will help you meet them where they are and then guide them toward academic success.

READ ALOUD

Read aloud to students … because they're never too old!

Reading aloud lets students fully engage their imaginations. Jim Trelease, author of The Read-Aloud Handbook, notes that a child's reading abilities don't catch up to their listening level until eighth grade. That means students will comprehend things they hear much more easily than things they read. Middle-grade students enjoy the process, which gives you another way to ensure engagement. Finally, since you can introduce books and information above your students' reading level, you'll inspire them to achieve academically so they can take up those books themselves!

Reading aloud can enhance socioemotional development. Trelease notes that he read to his daughter during her turbulent tween and teen years to help her find an anchor. Listening to someone reading aloud provides a calm, relaxing atmosphere in which students can remove themselves from the active role demanded during so much of their day. The fact that they're learning while decompressing helps your entire classroom!

Read aloud on a consistent schedule. Select shorter novels, so you can switch between different types to reach every child. You can also slip in essays, opinion pieces, or memoirs that tie into the curriculum. Be sure to give volunteers the opportunity to read aloud! You'll encourage natural performers and free yourself to catch up on paperwork or other details.

PLAN FOR THE END

Plan for the end of each lesson to enhance retention and improve engagement.

Plan for the end gets your students directly involved with their education. This type of closing method reviews the day's lesson and cements what's been learned. It prepares for the next lesson by adding to the educational foundation and encourages questions that might linger in a child's mind.

Plan for the end is advocated at institutions like Cornell University and among academic publishers like Scholastic. Ann Sipe, a teacher in Washington State, recognizes the value of planning for the end. She found 40 ways to wrap up a segment by asking students to write about what they learned, how the lesson relates to their lives, and how they might use that knowledge in the future.

Plan for the end by passing this responsibility to your students. If you provide the wrap-up, they're passively listening. Engage them directly by having them write a short paragraph about the lesson. Break them into small groups and have each group list three things they learned. Ask them to share how they might use that information in their lives. Pair students off with a buddy and have each child explain one component of the lesson. By engaging kids with the lesson plan every day, they build their own academic foundation!

FAIL FAST, FAIL OFTEN

Fail fast, fail often allows for missteps in the educational path while renewing a student's desire to try again.

Fail fast, fail often gives you and your students a little breathing room. It redefines success as an outcome that results from an effort. You know that children will never reach the right answer all the time. Success comes from the fact that they've made a real attempt to learn. If they fail to find the right answer, new success comes from a repeated attempt. When they fail fast and often, morale stays high!

Fail fast, fail often takes a lot of the fear out of the school environment. So much of a student's day is regulated by clocks, rules, and expectations. By the time they actually sit down to work, they might be anxious because of something their peers said or an adult's judgment. The last thing they need is to feel like they've failed utterly when they don't get the right answer! By allowing them to fail fast, you encourage them to move beyond an incorrect answer. Encouraging them to fail often motivates them to try new things. This is the core of the educational experience!

Fail fast, fail often by eliminating shame. No one is allowed to make fun of someone who gives an incorrect answer. Update students about their progress on a regular basis, so they can see the visible results of their constant effort. Clearly let them know that in your class, success is readily achieved because any real effort is a success. Everything else comes with time!

TEACH BEYOND THE TEXTBOOK

Teaching beyond the textbook connects students to the curriculum in ways that are relevant and exciting.

Teaching beyond the textbook nourishes learners. It provides students with a positive self-image and engages their strengths. They recognize that they can learn and that the curriculum in the textbook applies to their lives. Best of all, teaching beyond the textbook allows creativity and inspiration to flourish!

Teaching beyond the textbook is supported by Carol Ann Tomlinson. She compares teaching only from the textbook to the time when mothers followed the advice of parenting experts. The parents became inconsolable when they followed a book to the letter only to have their children act differently than the children in the book! The same thing can happen in a classroom when teachers follow the textbook to the exclusion of all other approaches.

Teach beyond the textbook by introducing new concepts. Teaching is all about connecting kids to the curriculum. If you need to discuss the finer points of SpongeBob to make your point, do it! Reach kids by allowing them to complete assignments in ways that fit their learning preferences. Utilize different teaching modes like reading aloud, performances, or drawing charts. You'll connect your students with a lifelong enthusiasm for learning.

TEACH GLOBALLY

Teaching globally provides a holistic view.

Teaching globally imbues your classroom with meaning. It provides a backdrop for lessons that focus on the interconnection of math to arts, of science to entertainment. It emphasizes the importance of human values within the learning environment and allows personal experiences to support and enhance academic achievement.

During the 1960s, the cultural paradigm shift focused more attention on *teaching globally*. Theorists who have championed this approach are as diverse as Jean-Jacques Rousseau, Ralph Waldo Emerson, Carl Jung, and Paulo Freire. The approach is truly timeless because it shows students who they are and how they fit into the larger world.

Teaching globally transforms the educational process. It modifies students' perspectives by providing them with a view of other topics, events, and ideas. Make connections by discussing the science of color as painters need to understand it. Link creative writing with history by studying the important social information found in classic books. Even when you're not linking across curricula, tie everything into the student's world by referencing modern issues and everyday challenges. When you teach globally, you prepare students to become citizens of our global society!

HOOK 'EM

Hook 'em by starting every lesson with an irresistible idea or activity.

Hook 'em makes your classroom an exciting place. It captures students right from the start of your lessons, giving you a strong hold on their attention. Your class, is therefore, much more likely to engage and stay engaged. And you'll have fun using your creativity to develop interesting hooks!

Hook 'em is a technique used by Dr. Julieanne Phillips. In an article for *Journal of Best Professional Practices*, she talked about the day she realized a hook's power. She was a sophomore in high school listening to her classmates present endlessly boring speeches. Then one student stood up and asked, "How would you like to go to hell?" He then gave directions to Hell, Michigan, as the introduction to his speech on highways.

Hook 'em using sensory input. Pass around flowers or essential oils to introduce a biology unit on the sense of smell. Play recordings of haunted house sounds to encourage descriptive writing. Pass around a piece of silk to discuss the science of tensile strength. Use a spiral shell to demonstrate geometric shapes. You can find virtual demonstrations of a variety of wonders online. When you hook your students on learning, you hook 'em for life!

FOSTER WITH FEEDBACK

Foster with feedback supports students with personalized contact.

Foster with feedback helps students learn specific lessons; it also helps them learn how to think. When you provide feedback, students discover exactly what they've done right and where they've gone wrong. They're able to improve over time, and this results in higher test scores!

Foster with feedback has long been an integral part of teaching. Recently, numerous studies have proven its effectiveness. Oxford University Press found that educators and administrators placed individual feedback among the top three things that would significantly improve the quality of teaching and learning. Because learning is naturally a trial-and-error process, constant feedback helps learners figure out how to improve.

Foster with feedback by keeping a few things in mind. First, be as specific as possible. Vague comments like "Not quite" aren't helpful.

Instead, point students to the problem by asking, "Could this step be done differently?" The University of Minnesota found that immediate feedback enhances comprehension much more than delayed feedback, so engage students in the moment. Encourage adjustments by letting them know that this change will help them reach their final goal. And, of course, be gentle with the budding personalities in your care.

HIGHER THINKING

Higher thinking skills—critical, logical, reflective, and creative thinking—lift your students to new levels.

Higher thinking skills locate answers by applying current knowledge. This type of success allows students to navigate the challenging world of education with confidence. When you encourage higher thinking, your students become more open-minded, flexible, and persistent!

Several states now measure *higher thinking* in their school assessments. Its primary definition is: reflection and inquiry that utilizes critical thought to produce a conclusion on the basis of more than beliefs and opinions. It doesn't rely on hard facts; instead, it requires deliberation on areas that are only hinted at by facts. With higher thinking, students rely on their intellect to tackle new challenges.

Support *higher thinking* by presenting students with situations that aren't clear-cut. You might introduce totally new information or throw out a paradox. Encourage critical judgment, creativity, logic, and problem-solving. At times you'll want students to work alone; at others, you can enhance the interplay of higher thinking skills with group discussions. When students feel they've reached a conclusion, have them argue their side in a debate, and have the class to vote on the most convincing presentation. Or have them list ways their conclusions might resolve a paradox. When they share that list with the class, you expose the entire group to thoughtful, critical analyses and creative solutions.

A FOUNDATION OF DIVERSITY

Celebrate *a foundation of diversity* to garner a host of benefits for your classroom.

A foundation of diversity strengthens every student's sense of self. It makes them more confident with their place in their peer group and enhances their independence. When diversity is honored and respected, incidents of bullying decrease. Relationships between students, and between you and each child, grow stronger!

A foundation of diversity can support your curriculum goals! Every time a lesson touches on a different nation, a historical time, or even stories from different subcultures inside the United States, point out how diversity creates new ideas. Changers and influencers come from every background and culture. When you point out how individuals invented, created, and led the way down better paths, you take students beyond the textbook and into the real world.

Build *a foundation of diversity* every day. A science lesson on light waves can note that many wavelengths, each of which registers as a different color, combine to create the brilliant light that allows us to see … just as diversity allows us to see fully. Writing and grammar lessons can be enhanced by pointing out words that originated in different languages. See if you can hook your classroom up with a "sister" class in some other country using social media. Daily posts can get students thinking about their own country and all the special people in it!

MONITOR TO MENTOR

Monitoring to mentor turns a task you do all the time—monitoring students as they work—into a tool that improves academic achievement.

Monitor to mentor is a hands-on process with immediate power. No matter how you monitor activities, you can step in when the challenge is difficult, provide praise as warranted, and assess ability levels.

Monitor to mentor combines two effective steps into one. Teachers monitor work to ensure that students are focused and engaged. Mentoring provides individual assistance to students who face challenges related to their abilities. When you actively monitor and mentor in the moment, you cut down on the need to reach out in other ways or at other times. You also encourage high performers to advance farther!

Monitor to mentor three easy ways. First, pick a day when you'll spend the entire time on your feet. Every time you task the classroom with an activity, meander down the aisles between desks. You'll be surprised how often your students will glance up and catch your eye with an expression that clearly asks for help! Other days, post yourself at different places in the room while students work. This makes it very easy for you to respond to hands or questioning looks. Finally, combine the two. Meander for a bit and then stand at different spots. Students will feel much more comfortable asking for help if you're close by.

LEAD A DEMOCRACY

Leading a democracy empowers students in their academic efforts and engages them more fully.

Leading a democracy steers clear of the controlling, restrictive dictates that crush creativity and discourage learning. When you share power with students, you support their intellectual and socioemotional education. Managing the classroom also becomes easier when students take control of their behaviors and efforts.

Johns Hopkins School of Education found that *leading a democracy* has a dramatic impact on responsible student behavior. They take charge of their own education and focus fully on achieving curriculum objectives. The key is that students respond well to individuals who build a collaborative environment. They become motivated and, when offered the chance to create their own rules, they shoulder responsibility for their behavior. They don't need a manager because they manage themselves!

To *lead a democracy*, remember that the social agenda is as important as the academic agenda. Children learn to process their emotions and react more appropriately when cognitive growth occurs in a social situation. Strengthen socioemotional and cognitive abilities by allowing the class to plan its activities during morning meetings. Guide children through the lessons and allow them to discover new things on their own and with the assistance of their peers. Make sure that the classroom is set up so that they can access the materials they need without having to come to you first.

CLASSIC CALM

Classic calm uses classical music to calm the classroom and enhance learning.

Classic calm calls on the powerful response people of every age have to classical music. Studies have found that classical music enhances verbal and spatial intelligence. Math students who regularly hear

Mozart while practicing are more focused and attentive. Any classical music reduces tension, anxiety, and inappropriate behavior. Classic calm is a simple tool that can be used every day!

Classic calm has such a powerful effect; it even impacts dangerous situations. In 2004, classical music was piped into London's underground train stations and certain neighborhoods with high crime rates. Vandalism, assault, and robbery dropped an astonishing 37 percent! While your students are far from hoodlums, you can reap the same benefits with the calming influence of classical music.

When using *classic calm*, avoid big crescendos and abrupt transitions like those found in Wagner. Mozart, Bach, Tchaikovsky, and Vivaldi are all good choices. Have the music playing as students first arrive to help them settle in more quickly. Hit the pause button to begin the lesson or during interactive portions and then resume playing while students work independently. When you repeat these steps every day, you'll automatically trigger relaxation, attention, and engagement in your classroom.

HANDS, PLEASE

Hands, please utilizes project-based methods to encourage active learning.

Hands, please helps you reach kids during that critical phase between kindergarten and high school when so many lose their passion for learning. It helps young minds grasp abstract concepts, connects ideas to the real world, and improves learning results. Because it can be used in any subject area, it's a perfect tool to boost academic achievement.

Hands, please has a long history in science and math because it has proven so successful in those areas. Concordia University found that the technique holds equal promise in social studies, history, English, and other subjects. The approach also fosters critical thinking, collaborative skills, and creativity. And since hands-on learning is fun, it's an almost guaranteed way to reach even the most reluctant learner.

Hands, please is all about active learning. Skip the lectures and dump the tests! Class trips to museums or space camps can take place in person or online. Create treasure hunts where each item ties into a different aspect of the lesson. Build a pyramid with paper cups. Assign each student to "perform" the role of a specific molecule and then have them stand so that they create a chemical bond … and then change the bond by adding new molecules. Hands-on activities are as limitless as your creativity!

SAFETY FIRST

Safety first involves your students in creating and maintaining a safe environment.

Safety first prevents the little accidents and mishaps that can derail plans and distract from learning. It comforts parents because they know that their child's health and well-being are well looked after. And it gives you confidence because even if something happens, the event won't spin out of control.

Safety first is supported by necessity through a school's regulations and procedures. But your classroom is like a separate world inside the campus universe. Every day is different, and you might engage in a number of activities that present new safety issues. The Center for Educator Development in Fine Arts, for example, defines the safe practices teachers should apply during arts-related activities. Each time you introduce a new learning aid, consider what students need to know to stay safe.

Safety first starts before you begin your day. Know all the evacuation routes from the classroom, the cafeteria, and other frequently used areas. Inside the classroom, keep things neat and free of clutter to prevent trips and falls. Always supervise students when they're using new equipment or items that present hazards. Never leave students unattended, even for a minute. At the beginning of the year, assign two students to each of these knowledge areas. Give them the responsibility of maintaining safety and you'll help students keep themselves safe!

SAFEGUARD VALUABLES

Safeguarding valuables ensures your day-to-day security and enhances your crisis response.

Safeguarding valuables keeps you from being disappointed when an unknown person steals from your personal items or classroom supplies. It also ensures that you'll be able to access important documents quickly if a crisis occurs.

Safeguarding valuables is an unfortunate step everyone has to take when they go into places where crowds gather. *The Student Teacher's Handbook* tells of a teacher whose cash was removed from her unattended purse while she guided students on a nature walk. Theft and destruction of property can happen because an individual needs certain things or because they want to lash out at an authority figure. And during a crisis, property and valuables can be destroyed by the event itself.

Safeguard valuables by leaving most of your property at home or in your car. Encourage students to use their lockers and bring only what they need into the classroom. Be sure your grades and other notes are backed up on a separate drive or in the school's network. To help students safeguard their valuables, be watchful when students are moving around or otherwise distracted. And never share code words or passwords; if you must, change them immediately after the other person is done accessing the files.

SPLASH AND DASH

Splash and dash harnesses the splashy effects of color, so your students can dash to success!

Splash and dash works because color triggers profound psychological and physiological responses. By thoughtfully integrating color, you'll help all students, including those with learning disabilities, perform at higher levels. You'll also be able to manage the atmosphere in your classroom more easily. When you tie color to the average age of your students, you'll reap even bigger rewards!

Splash and dash is being used in a variety of institutions. Law enforcement has found that pink reduces aggression in inmates and detainees. Red is used by restaurants to increase the amount of food people eat and to enhance sociability among diners. And since light waves are absorbed by the skin, several studies have found that color can impact the blind!

Implement *splash and dash* by recognizing that vast swaths of color can be as over stimulating as a busy pattern. Too much color can distract the mind as it constantly tries to organize visual information. For younger kids, age 7 to 11, use red, blue, and yellow. Older students respond well to orange, violet, pink, and brown. Avoid black and gray because of their negative connotations. The calming effects of green can be a teacher's best friend!

YOUR STUDENT FAMILY

Your student family builds an environment in which students can treat each other with familiarity and trust.

Your student family creates a supportive atmosphere inside the classroom. Incidents of bullying will decrease, and kids will be more likely to help each other with academic and social challenges. You'll enhance their sense of identity by encouraging them to grow with others. And you'll help them develop in conjunction with their peer group by encouraging positive interactions with fellow students.

Your student family has been discussed in *Psychology Today* magazine. In one article, Dr. Carl Pickhardt tackled social cruelty so that teachers, administrators, and counselors could reduce bullying in the place where it's most likely to occur. Making school a safe place enhances learning opportunities because scared and guarded children are closed even to adults.

Build *your student family* by focusing on your classroom community. Find the things that many students have in common and integrate them into your lessons. Encourage sharing of ideas, supplies, and equipment by having students work cooperatively. And when one child faces a challenge, let the entire class know that this challenge is common to his or her age or grade. When you find and enhance the commonalities, you create and support a student family!

SPEAK SLANG

Speaking slang allows you to keep up … and to help students with their communication skills!

Speaking slang allows you to interpret the everyday language students prefer. Since children tend to address teachers in much the same way they talk to each other, you'll understand them better. When you know exactly what they want to say, you can adjust their communication skills to language that relies less on slang. And if you overhear something other teachers missed because they don't know slang, you'll be able to step in before things get out of hand!

Speaking slang might mean that you have to learn universal and regional slang terms. One teacher in New York's South Bronx noted that her students' slang was highly localized. The Bronx localisms they used were a matter of pride. But overuse might have impacted their reading scores and set them behind peers in other schools. By learning their language, she helped them excel.

Learn to *speak slang* by checking out websites like InternetSlang and UrbanDictionary. For slang used in texts and e-mails, try NoSlang or NetLingo. If you've come across a specific term and need to know what it means, just search for the term's definition. Encourage students to use Standard English by interrupting them often to ask for a "translation." To really have fun, have them parse sentences written in slang!

INTERACTIVE CLASSROOM

Interactive classrooms ensure that every student will read, write, and speak at some point every day.

Students learn best when they participate in the acquisition of knowledge. An *interactive classroom* helps them solve problems and engage with lessons. The application of concepts deepens learning and higher thinking skills boost retention. By constantly refocusing attention on the work, you cause their efforts naturally to become more efficient.

Interactive classrooms, according to Brown University's Sheridan Center for Teaching and Learning, help students articulate what they discover. When students engage in interactive activities, teachers are better able to judge how well students are learning. That judgment allows for precise adjustments to the amount and type of assistance each individual receives.

Create an *interactive classroom* by integrating short, simple exercises like entry and exit tickets. After students have reviewed text or materials, ask them to write down a few quick sentences that explain the topic. When the lesson is over, ask them to write a sentence or two about what they learned. You'll receive a snapshot of the lesson's impact, discover target areas that need review, and determine which students might require help.

ESTABLISH ROUTINES

Establish routines to define expectations and boundaries within which students are free to succeed.

Establishing routines creates efficiency in a situation that—kids being kids—has the potential to become chaotic at the slightest opportunity. Routines establish guidelines and boundaries that make students feel safe and secure. Children crave predictability. Providing them with a specific landscape in which they can explore frees them from worries about doing something wrong!

Establishing routines can have a tremendous impact. Do remember one point made by the Center on the Social and Emotional Foundations for Early Learning: routines are not the same as schedules. Schedules create a big picture, and the goal is represented by the activities planned for a specific day. Routines are the steps by which those goals are met.

Establish routines early in the year. Students come from a variety of backgrounds and they've followed other teachers in the past. Your preferences aren't going to be exactly the same as anyone else's. Tell students how you want them to enter the classroom and what they should do to prepare. Tell them what they should place on their desks at the start of every day. Write a prompt on the board before they arrive, so they can begin working the minute class starts. You'll be surprised how much easier it is to get everyone settled if the lesson is already waiting for them!

ARRANGE THOUGHTFULLY

Arrange thoughtfully to maximize learning and minimize distractions.

Arranging thoughtfully helps you manage student behavior by manipulating the physical environment. Changes in seating arrangement can shift the class from task-oriented activities to more socially supportive activities. Thoughtful adjustments can also reduce visual and auditory distractions that might disrupt focus.

Thoughtful arrangements spring out of a variety of simple steps. The Classroom Management & Culture Toolkit available online from the Resource Exchange (TFANet) notes that a classroom's efficiency can be impacted by: displays on the bulletin boards, the placement of learning centers (spaces dedicated to certain types of activities), and the orientation of desks to each other, the teacher, and the board.

Arrange thoughtfully by ensuring that every student has a clear view of you! This also gives you a sight path to each of them. Set up traffic patterns that reduce the number of students near high-use areas like the pencil sharpener and trash bin. Cordon off a space where students can work at a quiet remove from the group. Encourage sharing by pushing desks and tables together; minimize interaction by separating desks into rows. Always, always provide a place to store unused possessions to reduce clutter.

MEET TOUGH WITH TENDER

Meeting tough with tender helps you break through the barriers tough kids build.

Meeting tough with tender is all about wiping away the past. Tough kids often walk into your class with a reputation a mile long. Don't let that skew your hopes for what might happen. When you give them room to grow beyond their tough-kid persona, you allow them to become everything they have the potential to be … and more!

Meeting tough with tender is a core focus for author and educator Allen Mendler. The books he's authored include *When Teaching Gets Tough, Discipline with Dignity*, and *Motivating Students Who Don't Care.* One day, he sat in on a conversation between a tough student and his teacher. The student wavered between constantly interrupting the class and refusing to engage with the lessons. Rather than hammer on the student, the teacher asked what he could do to help him become a better student. The boy was so shocked by the approach that he actually made some suggestions!

Meet tough with tender in your attitude. First, welcome tough kids warmly and avoid signals that you'd rather they be in someone else's class. Let them know you're ready to try new things … and that you are open to hearing about how your actions can help. Rather than demanding that the student change, ask what you can do to help them learn. By including them in the process, you're much more likely to discover a path the student is willing to walk.

TACK AND TRIM

Tack and trim takes advantage of changing circumstances like a sailboat gliding over the ocean.

Tack and trim is inspired by a quote by Elizabeth Edwards: "She stood in the storm, and when the wind did not blow her way, she adjusted her sails." In education, you don't adjust only when the wind blows against you; you adjust all the time! When you're quick to take up new ideas and pursue new opportunities, you enliven your classroom and energize learning.

Tack and trim is a strategy used by highly effective teachers. Teaching as Leadership proved this when they studied how best to fit lesson plans to specific timeframes. They found that when time runs out, the plan was usually too ambitious. On the flip side, when time was left over, the lesson might not have been challenging enough. Tack and trim helps you tailor the work to the boundaries of the classroom experience.

Tack and trim reaps big rewards on the fly. Sometimes students can be distracted by an upcoming holiday or special event, so capture their interest by connecting parts of the lesson to that special day. If students are puzzled at the end of a lesson, let them work together on a new challenge that teaches the same lesson. Switch to a different learning mode or back into the solution with a top-down approach. Tack and trim helps you use whatever works in the moment!

TAKE TEN

Take ten to find a convenient, efficient way to keep your classroom operating at maximum efficiency.

Take ten to integrate recurring chores into the flow of your day. Your classroom and work space will remain clean and clutter-free. You'll utilize small units of down time that might otherwise slip unused through your fingers. And since recurring chores are often tedious, performing the tasks in multiple smaller steps means they get done with a minimum of fuss.

Take ten is a ten-second activity that moves you that much closer to completing a task or chore. In the normal flow of your school day, you'll find a multitude of ten-second windows. The pause when students are settled into individual assignments is one; the time when you're making your way back to your desk is another. Every small window of time becomes an opportunity to catch up, clean up, and keep things operating smoothly!

Start by looking around for chores that fall into the *take ten* category. A bookshelf, a supply storage area, and the corner of your desk where small tasks pile up are all good candidates. Whenever you find yourself with a tiny window of time, straighten one item on the book shelf or in the supply area. Perform one small element of the task at the top of your to-do list. Even something as simple as entering a single grade into your record can move you forward. As you chip away at the smaller things throughout the day, you'll find that your end-of-day tasks consume less time!

LEAP IN!

Leap in encourages you to engage in the same activities as your students.

Leaping in conveys a direct message to students: the tasks you ask of them are important enough for you to participate! When you perform the same activities or join one of their groups, you're also building relationships on a whole new level. And because leaping in involves a little play acting, you'll discover your own sense of fun.

Leaping in can have a positive effect on learning. Rather than simply asking questions, you can say, "It's my turn now," and respond to a question from a student. Because you've taken a question from the group, you will probably clarify a specific point that was confusing. By allowing the question to arise this way, students might pose a question they otherwise would be too embarrassed to ask.

Leap in by engaging in the lessons at least once a week. Sit with a small group and work on the same level as the students. It's important to clearly relinquish control, so nominate a leader by asking one of the students, "How should we begin?" When you assign reports or essays, share one that you've created to fulfill that task. After a test, offer thoughts about the difficult questions to encourage students to discuss the snags they stumbled over. The entire time, you'll glean new information that can assess progress among individuals and the entire class.

Part III

Essential Knowledge for Yourself

YOUR TRUE CALLING

Your true calling is the single life path that fills you with enthusiasm, sparks your passion, and keeps you going through the down times.

When teaching is *your true calling*, you do whatever it takes for your school to succeed. Parents pick up on your passion and are inspired to help wherever they can. Students mirror your enthusiasm with their own efforts. Peers recognize you as a role model and administrators value your dedication. You become a central figure when you follow your life's best path!

LeAnn Morris, a K-5 technology teacher in Carson City, proved that teaching is her *true calling* when she became Nevada's Teacher of the Year. She was inspired by her Grandmother Wille, who taught in a one-room schoolhouse in Steamboat Springs, Colorado, during the 1920s. This role model and a series of teachers had an impact on Morris early in her life. The effect must have been profound because she went on to pursue a Ph.D. degree in Education!

Nurture your *true calling* by recognizing the place you hold in today's society. The future of our nation depends on the work you do every day. The gift you have—to encourage those who struggle with lessons, kids who are unsupported at home, and peers who face their own difficulties—sets you apart. You make a difference simply by following your heart!

PLAN FOR YOUR BEST

Plan for your best sets your goals anew every day and keeps you focused, passionate, and powerful!

Plan for your best reminds you what all your efforts are really about. When you think about your goals for your career, your students and your school, you are able to see the steps needed to achieve those goals. And when the smaller milestones don't arrive as quickly as you'd like, you can recharge your enthusiasm by recognizing how far you've already come.

Planning for your best will take different forms depending on each of your goals. When you're looking to enhance student participation, call on students in rotation until every individual has provided feedback. If your goal is to integrate one of your creative aptitudes into your teaching methods, role-play with students, so everyone can learn about a historical period. Even the simplest plan can have a big impact!

Plan for your best every day. When you first arrive at school, take a few minutes to consider your primary goal for that day. Jot down a reminder on a sticky note and post the note on your desk. Keep the reminder short, just a few words that encapsulate your goal. Every time you return to your desk, you'll be reminded of the day's goal. You'll continually implement actions to move you closer to that goal.

REMEMBER WHO'S IN CHARGE

Remembering who's in charge empowers you despite the obligations mandated at local, state, and federal levels.

Remembering who's in charge places you in the driver's seat. When you step up to the command post, you keep students engaged with lessons that inspire their minds and their passions. You feed your own passion and display an approach that others can mimic. By taking charge, you automatically ease the burden on the principal and other administrators. And this generates new opportunities for your career!

Remembering who's in charge has a healthy, active role in school. The *Washington Post* reports that at least 70 public schools in 15 states are run by teachers with at least 10 more teacher takeovers planned. When the learning process is redesigned this way, academic performance increases and the new teacher dropout rate decreases. School rankings also rise, even when a school receives less money per student than neighboring facilities.

Remember who's in charge by lobbying for a teacher advisory panel at your school. Allow administrators to perform most management functions to keep your workloads balanced while engaging the panel with all decisions. Even if your group can't actually run the school, principals and staff will be able to perform their jobs better. Having access to your expertise, experience, wisdom, and ideas will benefit everyone on campus and the community!

TEACH FOR A HIGHER PURPOSE

Teach for a higher purpose introduces a spiritual component that floods your days with light!

Teach for a higher purpose integrates an overarching purpose into your efforts. You'll still follow your heart and strive to achieve state and federal mandates ... but you'll do so with a loftier goal in mind. Keeping your eye on that special prize allows you to negotiate difficulties with less stress and elevates your activities with joy.

Teach for a higher purpose fits hand-to-glove with education. The children in your classroom today will become the leaders of tomorrow. The National Association of Secondary School Principals (NASSP) found that higher goals drive instruction, differentiation, and assessment in quality teaching. Just as sharing the goal of a specific lesson compels students to work harder and engage more, consciously setting a higher goal for your efforts spurs you to greater heights!

Teach for a higher purpose by considering why you chose the profession of teaching in the first place. So many of us want to inspire a love of learning that becomes a lifelong habit. We know how important academic achievement is to innovation, and so every building block handed to a child creates his or her future. In addition to leading students forward, we also want to lead peers and parents toward that same future. Using components from all of these drivers, create your own mission statement. Use your mission statement as a screensaver to inspire yourself anew every day!

BLAZE YOUR TRAIL

Blaze your trail according to what lies within you … not what lies behind or ahead of you.

Blaze your trail is inspired by this quote from Ralph Waldo Emerson: "What lies behind us and what lies before us are tiny matters compared to what lies within us." No matter what external pressures you face—budget cuts, large classrooms, aging facilities, or a fractured community—your inner resources are the solution!

Blazing your trail can have a profound impact on academic success. The Arts Education Partnership (AEP) found in study after study that students who engaged with the arts showed significantly higher reading and math scores immediately and over the long term. Programs were brought to different schools by creating partnerships with existing theater groups, independent artists, and other creatives in the region. By blazing a path past the funding issues and into new territories, teachers were able to lift their students in many ways.

Blaze your trail by utilizing everything at your disposal. Look beyond the usual in-school resources to discover new treasures that are yours for the asking. Reach out to parents, small businesses, and local nonprofits whenever you want to do something the budget or current resources can't support. When you blaze trails, you pave the path to academic success!

HEALTHY TIME-OUTS

Healthy time-outs maintain your balance and reduce your stress.

Healthy time-outs apply to your physical and psychological well-being. When you're sick, stay home so that you can return to the classroom rested and refreshed. When your emotions are off balance, a healthy time-out will reduce your stress and give you a new perspective.

Healthy time-outs are a teacher's best friend. Tracy Mercier, a classroom consultant, champions time-outs as a way to help students self-regulate. She encourages teachers to implement time-outs with students before they hit full meltdown mode. By catching the emotional whirl early, teachers can help students become more aware of where they're heading before they go nuclear. The same approach works for teachers in the classroom … and you might find that it's useful in your personal life, as well!

Healthy time-outs can take anywhere from a few seconds to a week or more. When you feel your temperature rising in the face of misbehavior, close your eyes and take one deep breath. Let it out to release the frustration. Then open your eyes and engage with the behavior in a productive way. To combat stress, take one minute while students are working independently to look out the window or gaze at a poster of a natural setting. Always plan a vacation during the academic year! Even if it's a staycation, knowing you'll have time to focus on yourself can help you get through the daily challenges.

THE POWER OF PASSION

The power of passion harnesses your love of what you do!

The power of passion is the engine driving your every effort. It is the creative force that allows you to find solutions to every problem. It is the thing that gets you out of bed every morning. Passion for your job carries you through the good times and the bad. It makes the difficult times easier while lifting you to new heights with every triumph!

The power of passion isn't some nebulous feel-good affirmation. It's a sound asset! Robert Fried, author of *The Passionate Teacher: A Practical Guide*, argues that most educational issues can be managed or even eliminated by passionate teachers. He proposes that teachers can be passionate about their field, issues facing the world, or children. Of course, many teachers are passionate about all three! All hold a philosophy based on a core set of values that supports learning.

Harness *the power of passion* by encouraging students to explore the curriculum in meaningful ways. Engage them with ideas and experiences that connect lessons to their world. Skip the rote memorization and provide challenges that build confidence and skills. Be their coach and their cheerleader! Set boundaries by communicating expectations as well as your disciplinary response. The power of passion can transform your classroom and everyone in it!

EVALUATE YOURSELF

Evaluate yourself empowers teachers by studying the effectiveness of learning.

Evaluate yourself puts the controls in your hands. In most schools, the emphasis is on external evaluations that come from principals, peers, or even parents. When you evaluate yourself, you consider how well your methods are reaching students. You pinpoint what works, understand why it works, and eliminate elements that aren't as effective. Evaluating yourself results in excellence!

Let's face it: teachers *evaluate themselves* every day of the year! You're constantly looking for new ways to address old issues and become more effective. When you consciously evaluate yourself, you undertake a planned approach that allows you to grow much more effective. Since you understand your students best, you are best able to adapt and adjust what happens in the classroom!

Evaluate yourself with several easy steps. First, document at least one success every day. Jot down the actual events that made this success a reality. Second, document one event that didn't go smoothly. Note the actual events that interfered with your ability to implement a successful lesson. As you progress with this tracking method, you'll find that some events occur regularly. When those events yield positive results, integrate them in a thoughtful manner. When the events create negative results, take proactive steps to eliminate them. Evaluate yourself to enhance educational achievement and ease your workload!

REFLECTIVE TEACHING

Reflective teaching is a process of self-observation that pulls data from a variety of sources.

Reflective teaching helps you slow down and consider the subtler things that might be overlooked in the crush of your busy day. Because you reach out to others to help you reflect on your methods, you'll discover new wisdom and fresh resources. You'll also avoid jumping to conclusions that, while they might make sense at first, turn out to be influenced by factors that have nothing to do with truly effective results.

Reflective teaching is systematic without being overwhelming. Something as simple as making an audio or video recording of one classroom session can allow you to consider moment-by-moment events that otherwise might be forgotten. Some teachers blog about different events, a form of self-reflection you can share with peers and other professionals. And when you include feedback from students, you add a new perspective that can help you reach everyone!

Reflective teaching can happen in a variety of ways. Record events in some fixed format, like the recordings or blogs noted above. As you review the record, consider how much time you spend talking compared to your students. Share your blog entries with teachers, administrators, and industry professionals to hear how they've solved similar issues. No matter what format you use, consider what you're doing, how you're doing it, the effectiveness of each step, and how you can make positive adjustments.

30/30

30/30 means don't teach your first year for 30 years. ... Instead, teach a new year every year!

30/30 keeps you engaged and inspired. It moves beyond the survival mentality and disillusionment that sets in for so many teachers during their first year and rejuvenates your attitude every time you plan another session. It allows you to continue learning and growing as an educator and as a person!

30/30 can make every year your best year ever! An article on Edutopia noted that professional development can help you achieve this goal. First, dive deep into all the courses. Go beyond what's required and discover what really inspires you. You can focus on your own academic field or dabble in new ones that intersect with your primary focus. Think systemically to supercharge your professional development!

30/30 is a lifelong career goal. Enjoy your work by focusing on positive experiences and professional milestones. Neuroscience tells us that the brain focuses on negative elements much more readily than positive ones. This makes sense; to survive, we have to avoid dangerous events. When you make an effort to focus on the positive, you become more relaxed and better able to handle stress. Connect with peers in your school and in other districts to garner and give support. Use these connections as new opportunities to focus on the positive aspects of teaching. This will keep you busy for decades!

BEYOND THE WALLS

Beyond the walls reminds you that an entire world awaits beyond the campus.

When you step *beyond the walls* of your school, you nurture the fullness of your own humanity. You engage in activities that expand your mind and enhance your soul. While you might bring those experiences into the classroom, your time outside the school is—and should—be about fulfilling the rest of who you are.

Beyond the walls is a critical element of self-care. Oxford's Department of Education found that in 2013, the average fulltime teacher worked nearly 60 hours per week. Their time was spent on the job with roughly 11 additional hours on preparation and planning, and nearly 10 additional hours on grading. With these kinds of realities, your life beyond the walls is critical to your health and well-being.

Optimize your time *beyond the walls* by seeking out activities and events that feed your mind and your soul. Your local arts organizations might offer discounted rates to educators … use them! Stop at a café on your way home for a cup of coffee out on the terrace. And be sure to nurture your body! Follow a regular exercise routine and treat yourself to a massage now and then. When you nurture the fullness of who you are, you bring your best efforts into the classroom.

FOLLOW THE SCHEDULE

Follow the schedule established by academic benchmarks laid out in state and federal mandates.

Following the schedule ensures that you comply with state and federal mandates. At the same time, it allows you to guide students through a process that builds upon the lessons that came before. When you engage creatively and critically with the curriculum, learning takes place on a deep level that impacts learners for life!

Following the schedule can feel like a teacher's worst enemy. Really, though, it can be your companion. Each core portion of the curriculum has a host of educational opportunities, which provides a great deal of freedom. You can opt for a chronological method one day and switch to a theoretical approach the next. No matter which teaching method you use, reaching across the individual lessons to achieve mandates systemically ensures that students retain what they learn. They'll also perform better when mandate fulfillment is measured!

Follow the schedule by focusing on the core areas to be taught. Then consider how each component might be presented. Try a storytelling format: the beginning presents the key issues and conflicts, the middle develops and explores the issues, and the end pulls together all the different components into a single narrative or solution. Follow the schedule to newfound freedom!

PREPARE EFFICIENTLY

Preparing efficiently gives you better control of your time and makes education much more productive.

Preparing efficiently reduces the time you spend on teaching-related activities outside of school hours … always a plus! Efficient preparation allows you to step into the classroom with calm confidence because everything you need is in place. You're able to focus on maintaining a productive learning environment without a million tiny distractions. Preparing efficiently means you no longer have to herd cats!

According to the State University of New York, *preparing efficiently* works best with moderate efforts. Robert Boice, professor emeritus of psychology, found that new faculty members achieve the greatest level of success when they slow down, begin work before they feel fully prepared, and break their efforts down into multiple small sessions rather than singular long sessions. Since this approach makes you calmer and more precise, it's a valuable approach for all teachers.

Prepare efficiently by allowing or asking others—students and peers and administrators included—to do some of the work. Be patient enough to slow lessons down when your class finds them difficult and flexible enough to speed up when their abilities allow. For all activities performed outside of the classroom, stop or at least take a break whenever you feel your quality of work is tapering off. Prepare efficiently and you'll automatically become effective!

LEARN LIKE A STUDENT

Learn like a student encourages you to never stop learning … about your profession, your school, your students, their families, and yourself!

Learn like a student helps you keep up with the constant flood of new thoughts, creative ideas, advances in knowledge, and changing information that rebuilds the foundations of our world. When you engage in lifelong learning, you model an attitude that values knowledge for the sake of knowledge. You inspire your students to reach higher, your peers to broaden their professionalism, and parents to engage in their own advanced education.

Learning like a student has a powerful impact in the classroom and beyond. Christa Portlock, author of *Foundations of Education and Instructional Assessment,* notes that in today's world, it's not enough to feed students information. Instead, we have to teach them to "fish for knowledge." The lessons don't stop at graduation … nor should they!

Naturally, *learn like a student* includes professional development opportunities. Beyond that, though, learning like a student can be fun! Attend theater productions, musical performances, and your city's annual arts festival to plug into creativity. Visit history and science museums (even ones set up for kids!) to discover things you never knew. Watch documentaries on streaming sites, read whatever catches your eye, and subscribe to at least one national newspaper. Every week, share at least one thing you've learned with your students to inspire lifelong learners just like you!

SPIRITUAL LIVING

Spiritual living supports everything you do as a teacher and a human being.

Spiritual living buoys you even in the darkest times. No matter what you face, you have a stable foundation that shelters you from the storm. When crises pass, you emerge knowing that you have endured and can continue on your path. A spiritual life—however you define spirituality—creates an attitude of gratitude! It allows you to appreciate all the beauty and wonder of your career and your place in this world.

Spiritual living has an impact on your classroom. In *The Courage to Teach*, Parker J. Palmer writes, "To educate is to guide students on an inner journey toward more truthful ways of seeing and being in the world." Teaching is all about encouraging students to make connections. Teachers are enthusiastic about learning and energize their students. They are creative and nurturing, and seek meaningful solutions that transform every child. This makes teaching a spiritual practice!

Live spiritually in the classroom by practicing wonder. Be curious about your students, their backgrounds, and their motivations. Nurture passion in their young hearts as fully as you nurture the intellect in their young minds. Guide them on their quest for understanding and nurture connections to their peers. Listen with your heart. You'll find that your already rewarding career choice has depths just waiting for you to plumb!

GROW LIKE A PRO

Grow like a pro encourages you to join organizations that enhance your professional abilities and support your career.

Grow like a pro demonstrates your commitment to your chosen profession. When you work outside the classroom to enhance your capabilities, everyone recognizes how serious you are. And when you expand beyond educational organizations, you'll spur your enthusiasm and discover new ideas. Growing like a pro makes teaching your life!

Grow like a pro is championed by the Association of American Educators. This nonprofit focuses on student achievement, teaching techniques, and other issues relevant to teachers, always with an emphasis on understanding that students learn differently. This same approach can help you grow like a pro. When you step outside the usual professional development classes and find organizations that introduce you to new ideas, you discover new opportunities for your journey as an educator.

Grow like a pro by casting a wide net. If your emphasis is in social studies, read widely from the world's classic literature to discover how stories are embedded in a particular place and time. Biology teachers will be fascinated by fractals, which have been called the math of the organic. Music instructors can use mathematics to understand and even teach music theory. Considering the wonders of our world, almost any organization that focuses on a different subject matter provides an opportunity to learn and grow like a pro!

INVEST FOR YOUR FUTURE

Invest for your future looks beyond your academic tenure ... even if you feel like you'll never want to retire!

Invest for your future is all about you. Teachers are a curious and enthusiastic bunch, so you'll want your retirement years to be filled with adventures and new challenges. The best way to ensure that you can continue to be a lifelong learner is to invest. You've spent your life building the futures of others. Now do the same for yourself!

Investing for your future is an important duty. The never-ending budget cuts that plague education have taken their toll on retirement plans and options for educators nationwide. *USA Today, Kiplinger,* and other leading finance publications have all looked at how difficult and confusing retirement can be for teachers. *Kiplinger* reported that a big part of the issue is that 403 plans, which are the norm for teachers, are handled differently than the 401s offered other types of workers. Little guidance or support is provided, so teachers are practically on their own from the start.

Take charge and *invest for your future!* Use 403bCompare.com, which was set up by a teacher's spouse, to review your options. Invest at least as much as will be matched by your employer as a first step. Then consider whether the rest of your investment capital might perform better elsewhere. Always compare fees because they can eat up your funds. Consider a Roth IRA and find an advisor you trust to set up a long-term plan.

NURTURE NUTRITION

Nurture nutrition to boost your performance and your career.

Nurturing nutrition helps you stay strong all day long. Quality nutritional choices feed your brain to keep you alert and focused. Your body will be stronger, so you'll catch fewer of the colds and flus that circulate at school. And when you're fit, you'll have the physical stamina required for classroom activities.

Nurture nutrition has a profound impact on your productivity. The World Health Organization (WHO) believes that adequate nourishment can increase productivity levels by 20 percent! Imagine if you were 20 percent better than you are right now. You would be more efficient, handle stress more easily, and be better able to help your students. And that would have a profound impact on your career.

Nurture nutrition by making healthy choices every day. Stash brain- and energy-enhancing snacks like protein bars in your desk drawer. Pack a bag lunch to ensure that the food you're eating is fresh. Remember that your executive judgment tires as you use it during the day, so plan a week's worth of evening meals ahead of time to avoid poor choices at the end of the day. If you constantly feel tired, ensure that your diet contains enough vitamins and minerals. Talk to your doctor about fatigue that doesn't go away; you might want to be tested for anemia.

RETIRE ON TOP

Retire on top encourages you to step aside when things are still going strong so you can continue to help others and yourself.

Retiring on top ensures that your students don't suffer when you naturally begin slowing down. It provides you with the freedom to branch out along new avenues that you just haven't had time to pursue. And since you can continue working to enhance your financial security during retirement, leaving while you're on top can open up an entirely different career!

Retire on top can be a tricky line to draw. You want to leave when you're still active enough to strike out in new directions but you don't want to contribute to the brain drain of experienced teachers by leaving too early. The National Bureau of Economic Research at Cornell discovered that when teachers were financially rewarded for retiring five years early (around age 55), test scores rose. The results were likely caused by new teachers who were open to the newest techniques performing better than less-energetic retirement-age teachers.

Retire on top and launch right into an encore career. Work part-time as a teacher or start another profession. You could even go back to school! Set up that freelancing business you've always dreamed about, write that book, record your memories as an educator, teach adult learners at continuing education organizations … the possibilities are limitless. Start thinking now about how you want to spend those golden decades!

ASK FOR HELP

Ask for help from your peers, school administrators, parents, and even students to ensure efficiency.

Asking for help takes some of the pressure off. When students help with classroom chores, the whole class takes responsibility for their environment. Your peers will feel good about helping coworkers, and assistance is the administration's top priority! When parents are called upon to help, they feel more connected to the school and strengthen community engagement.

Teachers in New York *asked for help* in a big way. Not too many years ago, their governor proposed reforms that would negatively affect evaluations. The changes included basing 50 percent of a teacher's evaluation on state test scores; another big chunk was to come from a single visit from an outside observer. Because the changes might have resulted in unfair firings, students were bound to suffer. The teachers turned to parents in a highly publicized request for help … and they got what they needed!

Ask for help by locating the person or people most able to provide assistance. Although some individuals might be willing to help, if their efforts won't be effective, don't waste your time. Instead, find the person with the authority to implement the change you'd like to see and go directly to that person. Start by laying out your request in a short but pointed e-mail or call. Follow up a few days later to ask whether they've had time to consider your request. You'll get help faster and your journey will be easier.

STOP AT THE END OF THE DAY

Stopping at the end of the day allows you to turn off the constant flow of thoughts, ideas, and plans so you can recharge!

Stop at the end of the day because a teacher's work is never done. … You just have to know when to rest! When you give yourself permission to turn it all off, you refresh your ability to think. You'll function at your optimal level. Your work will flow more easily and your stress level will decrease!

Stopping at the end of the day can be particularly challenging for teachers. Ileana Jimenez, a leader in social justice education, supports the use of teacher sabbaticals as a form of self-care. Longer leaves can also be used to conduct research that will enhance a teacher's performance. Sabbaticals are so important that Jimenez believes schools should offer them to enhance retention rates!

Stop at the end of the day by managing your time. When parents need to talk but can't make time during the work day, encourage the use of e-mail for all but emergencies and regularly scheduled conferences. Step outside of the classroom physically and mentally to engage in a fulfilling world. Follow a regular exercise schedule, treat yourself to a massage, and take lots of nature walks. Stop every day and you'll start fresh every morning!

BE CHOOSEY

Being choosey empowers you to select each step along your path … and to choose a different path when the time is right!

Being choosey puts you in charge of the classroom today. It also makes you the guide for your students' future lives. When you make conscious choices about procedures, methods, and goals, you pave a specific pathway for your kids. And since you walk that path with them, every choice paves the way for your career!

Being choosey starts with your decision to enter teaching as a profession. You chose a particular subject or grade level as your primary focus; every day you choose how to implement the curriculum mandated by your state. You choose when to discipline and how to reward. You choose the people who receive your respect and how to deal with those who don't deserve your respect. When you choose, you step into your power!

Be choosey by gathering the information you need to make a strong choice. At times, a peer or trusted confidant can be your sounding board … and you might choose different peers to help you parse different issues. Reflect on how different choices can benefit your class, your career, and your school. No matter what you choose today, you can always choose something different tomorrow! The power is yours because the choice is yours.

HIT THE EDGE

Hit the edge by constantly enhancing, revamping, challenging, and consuming!

Hitting the edge challenges your students and enlivens your classroom. When you move along the edge, you lift your school in the eyes of your community and in national rankings. Your efforts invite parents and other community partners to support academic achievement. And when you consume at the edge, you challenge and enliven yourself!

Teachers across the nation *hit the edge* every day. Whenever you read an article about a teacher who goes above and beyond to find the resources their class or school needs, you're reading about someone who has hit the edge. The teachers known for being creative about their procedures and lessons are working at the edge. When you hit the edge yourself, you discover new ideas, activities, and information that lift you above your current methods!

Hit the edge in your classroom by inviting students to decorate using pictures, photos, or sayings that are meaningful to them. Revamp lessons by teaching the same curriculum in inventive ways. Challenge your students by having them teach their parents something they've learned! Consume everything that tickles even a little of your interest. Hit the edge and you'll be ahead of the game in every way.

CUT IT OUT

Cut it out slices through all the small annoyances, petty issues, and weighty burdens.

Cut it out clears the path ahead. When you let go of little grievances that don't really matter, you clarify your attitude toward your school and your peers. When you trim away the petty issues that keep others mired in the mud, you become more effective and efficient. And by leaving unnecessary burdens behind, you advance more quickly along your chosen path.

Cut it out is never more appropriate than at school. Every day, it seems, teachers are met with a host of issues from demanding parents, challenging students, faltering peers, and clumsy rules. When you slice free of those bonds, you release yourself from the shackles that hold you back. Your attitude becomes confident, and every action becomes crisp and effective!

Cut it out first and foremost by practicing forgiveness. Recognize that we all occasionally say things we don't mean … and we all say or do things that are unintentionally hurtful. Next, cut away any burdens you've carried in from outside school. You'll have time to focus on those challenges later; right now, the students are the most important thing in your sight. Finally, step away from the baggage … especially if it's not your own! Be supportive of others but when their griping gets to be too much, excuse yourself. You have more important things to do. Cut it out and let them carry their own weight!

GRATITUDE IS GRACIOUS

Gratitude is gracious because it places you in an emotional state of grace.

Gratitude is gracious is an emotional response that is so profound, several world religions have chosen it as a core focus. Gratitude reinforces prosocial behaviors and so can be an important motivator in the classroom. A wide-ranging body of studies determined that gratitude graces individuals with a stronger sense of well-being in their lives and relationships. The graciousness of gratitude has a place in every teacher's toolkit!

Gratitude is gracious for teachers in part because teaching is often called a thankless job. Really, nothing is further from the truth. Thanks come every time a student achieves a new milestone and their eyes shine with triumph. Thanks come from parents who trust you enough to let you do your job. It arrives in the easy smiles of your peers and the confidence of school administrators. When you are gracious enough to recognize these many forms of thanks, your gratitude allows you to shine!

Allow *gratitude to make you gracious* by keeping a gratitude journal. Every day, jot down one positive thing that happened. Don't limit yourself to the classroom or academic activities! You might have noticed how well the groundskeeper makes things look in front of the school. The break room might have been particularly quiet or a peer shared a fun moment with you. No matter what happens, if the sun is shining, gratitude will make you gracious!

EMBRACE THE JOURNEY

Embrace the journey because your very special profession offers a lot of life lessons!

Embrace the journey frees you to accept whatever might have happened in the past. It gathers everything you have today into a huge pile of blessings. And it turns you toward the future, a place that shines with the promise you are already on your way to fulfilling.

Embrace the journey that is a teacher's quest. Your career is so much more than a job! You hold the lives of the next generation in your capable hands. You have a profound impact on the present world and on the future in which we will all live. Every hour of every day, your actions and ideas improve the quality of life for your students, their families, your school, and the nation. Embrace all that you do to embrace this precious journey!

Embrace the journey by honoring your special path. Only certain types of people dedicate themselves to educating our youth, so your choice has singled you out. Release any regrets about past activities because every one of them, good and bad, has made you who you are. Accept all the joy and fun of today by allowing others to be who they are in all their goodness and in their less-than-perfect ways. Rejoice in the future you are building for yourself and everyone else!

BE FAIR

Be fair by making sure everyone gets what they need … including yourself!

Being fair allows you to tailor your approach to the needs of the students in your classroom. It ensures that different types of parents receive the support and advice that helps their children succeed. And it allows you to assist peers with their careers while opening opportunities for you to get what you need!

Being fair extends far beyond the classroom. New teachers naturally need more counseling and support, so it's fair to provide them with more attention than is provided to teachers who are already established. Similarly, you might have to spend more time talking to parents who've just moved to the area or whose children are new to your school. It's fair to help them more than others because that's what they need to succeed!

Be fair not by providing everyone with the same effort or time but by providing what each individual needs in the moment. Tailor your interactions so that every person can succeed. Along the way, you'll discover that those individuals will be much more likely to reciprocate when you have a specific need. When you help others succeed, you help yourself succeed!

STARSHINE

Starshine reminds you that we can't recognize how brightly stars shine without the surrounding darkness.

Starshine helps you stay the course. Challenges are many and are never far away in the academic world. Even in the darkest night, though, you only have to look up to find millions of tiny points of light. If you keep your eyes on those sparkling lights, they'll guide you until the new day arrives.

Starshine helps with one of the worst difficulties teachers face: self-doubt. Ellie Herman, a teacher-turned professional tutor, told The *Washington Post* that teachers' doubts often stem from external factors. Education is in such a deep crisis, and has been in crisis for so long, it can be difficult for educators not to wonder if they're failing. Whenever these little monsters cast their shadows, keep your eyes on the starshine!

Enjoy *starshine* by cultivating a sense of gratitude. When you recognize all the little things that steadily provide comfort and support, you realize how big a sum that truly is! Maintain an attitude of peacefulness, so you're always able to find those little stars. And if ever you doubt your abilities or capabilities, peek into your classroom. Every face is a developing star that shines because of you!

GOOD TO GO

Good to go allows exercise and physical activity to keep you alert in the classroom.

Good to go impacts your physical health and your mental well-being. When you stay physically fit, you're better able to meet the demands of leading a classroom full of young children! And because you'll be less stressed, you'll become more patient.

Good to go addresses some of the top challenges facing teachers. Ken Mrozek, author of *Teacher Stress*, found that 33 percent of new teachers quit before their fifth year due to stress. Exercise has been found to reduce stress across all age groups and fitness levels. Something as simple as a ten-minute walk can lower your blood pressure and help you focus. Since it also boosts the endorphins that enhance mood, staying physically active is truly your best friend!

Stay *good to go* by doing something active every day. Although teachers are on their feet most of the day, they're not getting the benefits of exercise. Standing or moving short distances doesn't elevate cardiac or respiratory rates, so they don't count. Start by adding a ten-minute walk around the school's property every morning. Then walk for another ten minutes at lunch or after you've gone home. Exercise doesn't have to be done in big chunks to provide big benefits. If you work in three walks a day, it provides three and a half hours of exercise every week!

BE HERE

Being here focuses you in the present moment, so you can perform at your highest ability.

Being here moves beyond the past. Any difficulties or obstacles, no matter how large they loomed, fade into the background. The triumphs you've enjoyed boost you to a higher platform from which you can spot new opportunities. The problems you might face in the future nag you far less, and the broad potentials that lie ahead develop more easily. When you stay in the present moment, you become everything you have the potential to be!

Be here to transform your teaching. An article in *Psychology Today* noted that when people are focused on the present moment, they enter a flow state. The sense of time passing disappears, as do any anxieties about schedules and obligations. Distractions have far less power to upset your train of thought, and the next step toward your goal becomes fluid. Being here makes you a powerful person!

Be here by acknowledging any issues that might be bothering you. Then acknowledge that you have done or are doing everything you can to address the issues. Accept that the outcome will be what it will be, and that you've done everything you can to create a positive outcome. This understanding allows you to release, relax, and engage in the present moment. The more you pay attention to the present moment, the easier being here becomes. Start today and soon you'll be here all the time!

SMILE

Smiling harnesses the power of your brain chemistry to move you into a happier, more positive state.

Smiling sends a message from the body to the brain. No matter what's happening, you can become more peaceful just by moving a few muscles in your face! The more you smile consciously, the more you'll smile without having to make a decision to smile. And in the crush of academic life, every smile is priceless!

Teachers who *smile* enhance the school environment. A genuine smile exchanged with other teachers or administrators makes their days brighter. Smiling at your students puts them at ease and makes them feel welcome. Smiling at parents comforts them and lets them know you're approachable. Every one of your many relationships can be enhanced with a simple yet powerful smile.

Smile when you're feeling down or lack motivation. It's a simple action you can do anywhere and for any length of time! To make that smile even more powerful, look in the mirror. Our brains have a certain process called mirroring, which means that we tend to feel the emotions others show. By looking in the mirror, you'll trick your brain into thinking you're interacting with a happy, positive person. In just a few moments, that person becomes you!

WORRY TIME

Worry time allows you to encapsulate problems and issues into a specific timeframe, so they won't intrude on the rest of your day.

Worry time gives you a realistic way to address issues. Everyone has problems, and ignoring them won't make them go away. But you don't want to spin in a constant vortex of anxiety. By allowing yourself a specific time and timeframe in which to worry, you give issues the attention they deserve without going overboard!

Worry time is an important classroom tool. Let's say you receive an e-mail from a parent that blows their child's problems out of proportion. The tone of the e-mail indicates that the parent is upset with the school, the curriculum … and by extension, you. It might not be fair or even something that's in your power to change, but you're the one they've contacted. Encapsulate this issue by placing it in your worry time folder. Then, during the five or 10 minutes you've allocated to issues, you can return to the e-mail and consider how best to move forward.

Set aside *worry time* as often as you need. If you set it up on a daily basis, you might be surprised how often you don't need the time! You'll also find that not every worry time runs for the full schedule. Both these discoveries will boost your mood. On days when you do need part or all of the worry time, you'll realize that having a scheduled time to focus on issues is actually quite freeing. Whenever anxieties try to creep into the rest of your day, you can push them aside because it isn't time for worries yet!

PLAY TO YOUR STRENGTHS

Playing to your strengths zeroes in on what you do well.

Playing to your strengths is the most efficient way to become an effective teacher. It keeps you focused on your natural talents and abilities, which makes you much more productive. And because you're using skills that are an inherent part of your makeup, you'll eliminate the stress that comes when you take up tasks that aren't suited to your skills.

In an academic setting, your career choice is set up to *play to your strengths.* You wouldn't have selected a certain area of focus if you weren't already good at it. Within that area, you know that some of your skills are stronger than others. When you apply those skills to other areas that must be done but at which you aren't as strong, you'll meet your obligations effectively.

Play to your strengths by applying your natural skills to your daily activities. You might be very detail-oriented, which makes you a natural for record-keeping, but be less able to connect with parents you see only occasionally. Use your detail-oriented nature to bolster your connections. Provide parents with details about their child's performance and behavior. Talk about their child's likes and dislikes, and how they impact the student's performance. When you provide these kinds of details, parents will feel more connected with you through the person you have in common: the student.

REVEAL YOUR TRUE SELF

Reveal your true self so that students and peers feel comfortable with the person you are!

Revealing your true self brings the human touch into your classroom. It makes students more comfortable because you aren't just an authority figure. Parents will trust you more deeply when they know that you have a rich, full life. Your peers will enjoy sharing things you have in common, and you'll feel more fulfilled.

Reveal your true self so that students will feel more comfortable asking questions. They'll learn how to interact appropriately with adults who are not their parents, and their behavior is more likely to align with your expectations. Even when your expectations are high—actually, especially when your expectations are high—students who feel like they know you achieve more!

Reveal your true self in bits and pieces. When you're teaching, share your own experiences learning the same subject. By sharing what worked for you, students learn new skills and coping mechanisms. When you discuss your early academic difficulties, kids discover that their issues can be overcome. You'll connect with your class in a way that makes them comfortable and that builds a pleasant environment.

INVEST IN THE DRESS

Invest in the dress turns your attention to how you present yourself every day.

Teachers who *invest in the dress* immediately convey their status as a professional to students, parents, peers, and the broader community. Because teachers are role models, students respect and appreciate those who dress for success. Proper attire places you first among equals. It sends a message to parents and the administration that you are a caring educator who focuses on every detail of your job!

Do an Internet search for "teachers who dress poorly" and you'll see why you should *invest in the dress*. Flip-flops, "immodest" clothing (and yes, fellows, that applies to you, too), t-shirts, overly loud patterns, sloppy shirts, wrinkled trousers … you name it, you'll find it. Comfort is important but so is the image you present to everyone in the school environment. Parents use the way teachers dress as a clue to the quality of the school. Students use it to figure out how to interact with each teacher. Do yourself—and your profession—a favor, and keep it professional!

Investing in the dress doesn't mean sacrificing comfort. Search for the right pair of shoes that look great and can be worn all day … and then buy them in black and brown. Have a quick and easy way hairstyle for workdays; you can always change it up on the weekends. Keep cologne and perfumes to a minimum, be spare with the jewelry you wear, and always have wrinkle-free basics in neutral colors to make mornings easier. With only a little investment of effort, you can ensure that you are always dressed to impress!

HIBERNATE

Hibernate to achieve the deep, quality sleep you need for peak performance!

Hibernating provides the rest your brain and body need to support your busy days. Although many Americans try to sneak by on six or fewer hours of sleep, most people need seven to eight hours. Proper rest decreases your health risks, increases your reaction time, and keeps you safe because you're alert enough to avoid accidents. Plus, you'll feel better!

Hibernation is the single biggest step you can take away from school to enhance your performance at school. Even better, being well rested allows you to deal with all the tiny annoyances that crop up in a typical day. Student misbehavior, unreasonable parents, strict mandates, and a host of other irritants fade in importance when your mind is refreshed and your body well rested.

Hibernate by preparing your mind and body for sleep every evening. Avoid any devices that emit blue light, the frequency that triggers your brain to maintain an alert state. If you must use the television, computer, or other displays right before bed, buy a pair of sunglasses with amber lenses. The blue light frequency that reaches your eyes will be significantly reduced, allowing you to wind down. And if you can, try to grab a ten-minute nap during lunch. Even that short bit of time works wonders to refresh your mind!

LEAVE A LEGACY

Leaving a legacy imbues your days with meaning.

Leaving a legacy as a teacher provides you with an important long-term goal. It supports new teachers during their tough first year and helps them during the next four years when retention rates are low. It keeps you going when the workload increases or your emotional burdens feel heavy. Legacy thinking propels you through the trials of burnout. Best of all, it affects the students you teach every day, year after year!

You'll know you've *left a legacy* when older students circle back to thank you for something you did. Every time a parent rejoices in their child's achievements and advancements, you'll recognize the legacy you're building for that family. Legacies might be marked by honors and awards; then again, you can mark your own milestones every time your grade level performs well in national testing. Best of all, you can see how the building blocks of your legacy stabilize the school and launch leaders in the world.

Leave a legacy by leading your students into their future. Share the wisdom you've garnered over the years with those young minds. Include not just academic lessons but the things you've learned as a friend, as a mentor and as a guide. When you leave a legacy for your students, you build a legacy for the world.

NETWORK NODES

Network nodes divide your contacts into groups that serve different purposes.

Network nodes allow you to categorize the people you know. When you consider how people are connected and the skills they possess, you'll discover new avenues that can ease your journey as an educator. And by moving beyond the typical categories, you'll develop relationships that go much farther than usual.

You already have *network nodes* set up among the people you know. These are the most basic: students, parents, peers, and administrators. Reaching out to these different groups locates volunteers for special activities, peers who can share their wisdom, and administrators with the authority to implement change. Each group offers unique skills and opportunities; taken together, they are a powerful force!

Expand the types of *network nodes* you have by considering the special abilities and connections individuals offer. Parents, for example, might have careers in fields that can benefit your school's academic or financial goals. Your peers might have come to teaching after working in different industries. Among your students, you might discover individuals whose creativity can enhance an afterschool or classroom effort. Network nodes recognize that every person possesses utterly unique abilities … and allows you to tap into new power and wisdom!

Final Words

Always a Teacher

Always a teacher means that your career isn't merely a job … it's a lifestyle!

Always a teacher means that you're always on task. Every person you meet has the potential to expand your network and help your school. Every book you read can somehow be utilized for your classroom. Even your vacations provide you with ideas and experiences that will spark academic engagement!

Catalina Fortino knows the meaning of *always a teacher*. In December of 2015, she received the Charles Cogen Award from the United Federation of Teachers (UFT). She was the UFT vice president for education and the director of their Teacher Center. Then she became UFT's vice president. She started her career in Brooklyn working as a special-education and bilingual teacher. Today she is a nationally recognized expert in several educational areas. Her lifetime of achievements resulted from always being a teacher!

When you take active measures to *always be a teacher*, your life expands in wonderful ways! Join a committee on your local teacher's union to help others and meet fellow professionals. A host of national associations, like the Association of Teachers of Social Studies, offer the same opportunities for teachers of different subjects. Reach out to local colleges and universities to see how you can help students find the path to higher education. And whenever you travel, drop in on local educator's groups to see how they do things! You'll grow, stay active and engaged, and bring the best to your students and your school.

About the Author

Barbara D. Culp has dedicated herself to education for 43 years. After teaching at the elementary and middle-school levels, she became the principal of a large elementary school and was selected as Principal of the Year. Currently, she is a part-time clinical supervisor for Brenau University's School of Education; she recently founded a tutorial service company for public, private, charter, and parochial schools. Dr. Culp graduated from Morris Brown College and Atlanta University with a master's degree and an education doctorate degree in administration and supervision. She has conducted workshops and training programs on classroom management and differentiated instruction.